SHOW ME HOW TO LEARN

Key strategies and powerful techniques that promote cooperative learning

ROBYN ENGLISH / SUE DEAN

Foreword by Katherine Luongo-Orlando

Pembroke Publishers Limited

To Evelyn Myers—my "teacher". Robyn

To the teachers and their students, who have made the difference to me.
To Ross—thanks. Sue

Pembroke Publishers
538 Hood Road
Markham, Ontario, Canada L3R 3K9
www.pembrokepublishers.com

Distributed in the U.S. by Stenhouse Publishers
477 Congress Street
Portland, ME 04101
www.stenhouse.com

Acknowledgement
The publisher would like to thank Queensland University Press for the permissiion to reproduce an extract, which appears on page 75 of this publication, from *Swashbuckler*, by James Moloney, published in 1999.

Show Me How to Learn was originally published in 2001 in Australia by Curriculum Corporation — www.curriculum.edu.au

We acknowledge the financial support of the Government of Canada through the Book Publishing Industry Development Program (BPIDP) for our publishing activities.

We acknowledge the Government of Ontario through the Ontario Media Development Corporation.

Library and Archives Canada Cataloguing in Publication

English, Robyn

Show me how to learn: key strategies and powerful techniques that promote cooperative learning / Robyn English, Sue Dean; Katherine Luongo-Orlando, editor. — Canadian ed.

Includes index.
ISBN 1-55138-178-8

1. Group work in education. 2. Learning. I. Dean, Sue II. Luongo-Orlando, Katherine III. Title.

LB1032.E55 2004 371.3'6 C2004-905023-0

Editor: Kat Mototsune, Ronél Redman
Cover Design: John Zehethofer
Cover Photography: Photodisk
Design: Catherine Squared Pty. Ltd., Jay Tee Graphics Ltd.

Printed and bound in Canada
9 8 7 6 5 4 3 2 1

Contents

Foreword

Children learn in dynamic ways. Just visit a classroom, playground, library or recreational program and observe young people at work and at play. Suddenly, you will notice a range of skills and learning behaviors that children use in their everyday world. Watching them interact with others, discuss topics, solve problems, use materials, create visuals, investigate surroundings and reflect on their experiences can be fascinating indeed. By observing children closely, we can see how they learn. With the help of this book by Robyn English and Sue Dean, teachers can show them how.

Show Me How To Learn recognizes the multifaceted ways that children learn. This practical resource is solidly rooted in implicit research frameworks, like Gardner's theory of multiple intelligences and Glasser's organization of human needs, along with other learning theories that provide the insightful underpinnings for the work of English and Dean. The authors provide instructional models and teaching strategies that support all students and reflect the range of learning styles of children in the classroom. The pages of this book are filled with teaching practices and educational tasks that will engage each type of learner.

- For the child who is fascinated with interest topics and enjoys reading nonfiction, the authors provide strategy lessons that show children how to locate data from different sources, take notes, organize information in a structured framework and develop important research skills in an authentic context.
- For the child who enjoys literature, this resource extends invitations to respond to reading through drama, readers theatre, retelling and reflective writing.
- For the child who likes writing, the authors include language tasks that help young authors understand the features of texts, develop vocabulary, construct sentences and communicate concepts effectively to others.
- For the child who uses reasoning, logical thinking and problem-solving to learn, this text provides schematic frameworks for classifying information, categorizing content and identifying relationships though comparison and contrast.
- For the child who learns through images, diagrams and pictures, the book features visual learning strategies that challenge students to develop graphics, construct charts and use concept mapping and other pictorial representations to organize their thinking and express their understandings.
- For the child who learns with others through collaboration and sharing, the authors provide practical guidelines for creating a successful classroom community and establishing independent learning centres where students can communicate and interact with others in cooperative groups.
- For the child who learns through self-reflection, metacognition and working alone, this resource describes assessment practices that invite students into the learning

and evaluation process. The student-led tasks, self-assessment tools and goal-setting procedures challenge learners to become fully independent, monitor their progress and make meaningful judgements about their work.

Show Me How to Learn embraces all children and recognizes their interests, needs and abilities. The authors illustrate how to create a successful learning community where students sense they belong, young people feel empowered, learners have control over their choices and decisions, and children experience joy in learning.

Through explicit instruction, modelling and practice, English and Dean provide students with lifetime strategies to learn and grow. The pages of this resource are filled with lessons designed to develop strategic language skills and promote higher level thinking. The frameworks, working samples and scaffolding techniques provided here will help both teachers and students create what Debbie Miller calls "working literate environments" in their classrooms and beyond.

Show Me How To Learn is a companion to other professional resources like *InfoTasks, Strategies That Work* and *Authentic Assessment* that share best practices with teachers. Like other practical books, this text extends invitations to educators to share their talents and develop their teaching practices. Let the authors show you how to enrich the lives of children in your classroom by imparting in them a genuine love and interest in learning. For Robyn English and Sue Dean, there is no greater gift a teacher can give.

Katherine Luongo-Orlando

Introduction

The notion of creating a learning community is something on which all teaching focuses. The idea of being a community, accepting individual differences, and striving to be the best we can be is a positive, lifelong process for adults and children alike.

Perhaps the most important aspects of teaching and learning are learning how to learn and reflecting on this learning in order to understand ourselves and others better. The love of learning is a great gift that we, as teachers, can create within a classroom by modelling and teaching reflective strategies.

Curriculum planning and the use of effective assessment practices underpin all teaching and learning within a classroom. Any experienced teacher will be able to share moments when classroom organization has been a bit lacking and how this affects learning and student outcomes. Looking ahead to plan, and then reflecting on practice and progress, are vital to improving student outcomes.

This book came about through the work that has evolved for us in our own classrooms. It has given us the opportunity to practise our reflective behavior, examining what we value as effective teaching, and how it all fits together. From our long discussions and "nutting out" sessions we became clearer on how teaching and learning fit together and how no one part is more important than another, but rather that the threads fit together to weave our educational communities.

We have aimed to produce a book of practical ideas that could be picked up by a teacher and put to work in the daily business of classroom organization. There is nothing more satisfying than flicking through a resource and instantly having something to try tomorrow or share. A positive outcome then builds a willingness to pick up more ideas.

Most of all, we hoped to achieve a practical set of guidelines for ways to create successful learning communities. Teachers have fantastic skills and knowledge which they often take for granted. If this text can give you a reminder or a springboard for strategies you have forgotten about, or ideas you can modify for your individual classroom, then we will have achieved our aim.

Author's Note

This book offers ways to organize and interrelate ideas that have been around for many years. It is important, then, that we do not claim these techniques and strategies as our own, but acknowledge the people who were instrumental in helping us gather ideas and build our learning community.

David Anderson and Joan Dalton (Hands On Consulting) have been an endless source of encouragement and professional stimulation. Their dedication to exploring ways to make children more effective learners has been inspirational, and with David's guidance we were able to develop effective goal-setting practices in our classrooms. Helen Newton, the leader of Roberts McCubbin Primary School, has been an admired friend and colleague. We thank her for her vision of what a school learning community can be, and her insight in bringing the authors together in a shared teaching environment.

We would also like to thank Denise Quinn and Wilma Culton for continuing support and encouragement as this book took shape.

1 Learning Communities

As educators, teachers want students to achieve their full potential in a positive environment. A learning community's core purpose is to create an environment in which students feel secure and free to learn. A classroom that has as its focus rules to control or govern may have success, but one in which students take responsibility for their learning and interaction within the room is more effective. If we value students and what they bring to the classroom, then we must value their sense of ownership of their education.

Working together to create an effective learning community is rewarding and professionally satisfying. If students are to face their future with skills and knowledge to continue lifelong learning, teachers must work with them to identify the rights and responsibilities of members of an effective learning community.

Establishing a Classroom Code

The lynchpin of an effective learning community is a shared and negotiated understanding of the ways in which learners treat one another.

The first task of a learning community is to establish a classroom code. This needs to be established cooperatively and agreed upon by all class members to ensure they share ownership and take on the associated responsibilities. Furthermore, the process needs to be seen as one that will continue to evolve over the year. It will involve a great deal of exploration and clarification through discussion, as well as individual reflection.

How to Create a Classroom Code

1. Individually, students list three ways in which they want to be treated while in the classroom. For example:

> *Three ways I want to be treated by everyone else:*
> - *I want people to listen to me when I say something.*
> - *I want people to share their things with me.*
> - *I want the teacher to treat us all the same. No favorites!*

2. Groups of three share their lists and add any suggestions made by others that they feel would strengthen their own lists.
3. Shuffle group membership so that new groups of three are formed. The new groups share their revised lists, add new suggestions and compile a new list.
4. It may be beneficial to repeat Step 3 several times to create comprehensive lists.
5. Come together as a whole class and generate a master list of all ways in which students want to be treated.

Collating the Code

1. Write each suggestion on a separate flashcard and display them all on a board so that they can be moved around.
2. Ask the students whether they feel any of the suggestions are related in any way, or whether any fit together into groups.
3. Manipulate list items into agreed clusters. This step will involve much student discussion and clarification of ideas. Although this is quite involved, it is a vital step towards shared understanding.
4. Create a suitable label for each subset of ideas.

Examples of students' suggestions collated into like groups:

> ***About sharing:***
> - *I want people to share their things with me.*
> - *People should share their belongings.*
> - *If someone has something you need to borrow, they should let you.*

> ***About responsibility:***
> - *Everyone should be responsible for their own things.*
> - *I want people to be responsible for their own behavior.*
> - *We should look after our own belongings carefully.*

About learning:

- *We should let all people in the class learn without distracting them.*
- *I want people to recognize my talents.*
- *The teacher should give us interesting work to do that isn't too easy or too hard.*

About friendship:

- *Everyone should be friendly towards each other.*
- *We all want to feel welcome in any group or activity.*
- *We should speak to each other in a friendly way.*

Exploring the Code

It is important to take time to provide the students with activities that assist them to work through the code items, understand what each one means and then explore the personal ramifications. The following suggestions give students the opportunity to do this. It is not necessary to do all the activities, but the extent to which the code items are explored through such activities will depend on the understandings that the students demonstrate. It is better to do more than not enough.

Pictorial representation

1. Write the code items as sentences on poster-size pieces of paper.
2. In pairs, students illustrate a classroom situation to demonstrate their allocated item. This shows what it **Looks like**.
3. Students then consider what it **Sounds like** by creating dialogue in speech bubbles on their pictures.
4. Display the posters prominently around the room to generate discussion and reinforce the agreed class code.

Y-Charts

1. Write each code item in a sentence on a poster-size piece of paper.
2. Underneath each sentence create a Y-Chart with the three headings: **Looks like**, **Sounds like** and **Feels like**.
3. As a whole class, complete one of the charts listing points to model the process to be used.
4. In pairs or small groups, students record their contributions to one Y-Chart.
5. Pass the Y-Charts to other groups or pairs to record their contributions.

6. Repeat Step 5 a few times to build a comprehensive set of points; however, be careful not to labor the process.
7. Display the charts prominently around the room to generate discussion and reinforce the agreed class code.

Sample Y-Chart:

In our learning community we will strive for effective oral communication.

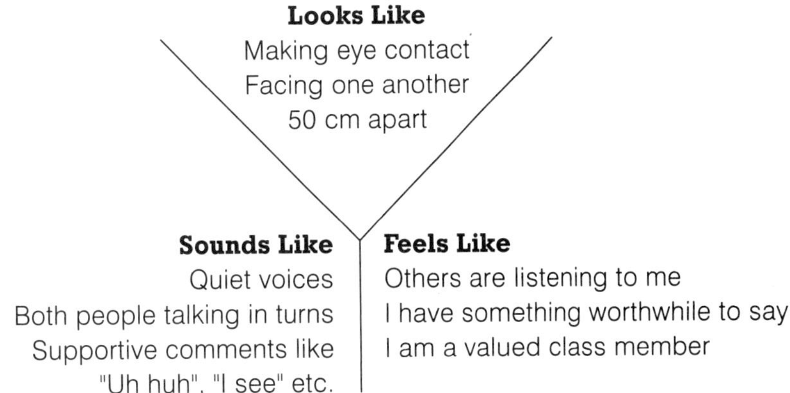

T-Charts

1. Write each code item in a sentence on a poster-size piece of paper.
2. Underneath each sentence create a T-Chart with the two headings: **DO...** and **DON'T...**
3. As a whole class, complete one of the charts listing words and actions that demonstrate the item. For example, listening to others, you **DO** "Make eye contact" and **DON'T** "Talk over others."
4. In pairs or small groups, students record their contributions to one T-Chart.
5. Pass the T-Charts to other groups or pairs to record their contributions.
6. Repeat Step 5 a few times to build a comprehensive list of points; however, be careful not to labor the process.
7. Display the charts prominently around the room to generate discussion and reinforce the agreed class code.

Sample T-Chart:

In our class community we will respect and value every other person.

DO	DON'T
• Speak politely to everyone	• Talk about others behind their backs
• Ask others for their opinion	• Spread rumors
• Take turns in discussion	• Use put downs
• Listen to others' comments	• Talk over the top of others

Note: There is the danger with the T-Chart strategy that students can over-emphasize the negative aspects of the **DON'T** behaviors.

Using the Classroom Code

Once the code is displayed in poster form around the room it can be used to keep the learning community focused.

- Returning to the agreed code at the beginning of each school term allows the class to settle quickly back into a routine. It serves as a reminder of the class expectations and sets the scene for the new unit of work to be covered.
- It can also be helpful to select one item as a daily or weekly focus. This will remind students of the agreed code and re-generate commitment to the behaviors determined by the learning community.

There will be times when the class is having difficulty, as a group, putting aspects of the code into practice. Individual students may also experience difficulty in behaving according to the agreed code. Having the code displayed around the room provides an appropriate and positive opportunity for the teacher to direct the students' attention to it and discuss issues or concerns. Thus, the teacher is enforcing behaviors set by the class, rather than dictating imposed rules. For example, groups of children who continually involve themselves in small discussions during instructional time can be drawn back to the agreed statement that everyone will demonstrate respect for each other. This will reinforce the understanding that such behavior does not respect the teacher's right to give instruction, nor does it respect the right of other students to receive tuition without interruption and distraction.

Sample of display poster for a weekly focus code item:

This week we are focusing on:

In our classroom learning community we respect everyone's right to have their skills and talents recognised.

Categorizing the Code

The code will differ from class to class and year to year. Regardless of the actual wording of individual items, commonalities will appear. Once all the items have been teased out and explored in detail, it is helpful to draw them together and find the similarities and common links.

Code items tend to fall within groups or categories. Glasser's organization of human needs is a useful tool to help teachers organize the codes into a manageable model. This model, shown below, acknowledges the physiological survival needs, but focuses on the needs of individual learners within a learning community.

Examples of Glasser's needs:

Belonging — Using class meetings to ensure students have the opportunity to air new ideas or problems they may be experiencing.	**Power** — Empowering students to move to a different working station in the room if they feel interrupted by students around them.
Choice — Providing a range of activities from which students choose.	**Enjoyment** — Using game situations for teaching.

SURVIVAL

Belonging—Students need to feel that they belong to the group, and to subgroups within the class group. As a member of the class, school and greater community, there is a sense of security in having personal membership of these groups.

Power—Students need to feel that they have control over their own learning and are in a situation in which they are empowered to act according to their beliefs.

Choice—Students need to have control over an increasing range of choices in their school lives. Options and choices, along with the ability to make appropriate personal decisions, are very important in developing individual and independent learners.

Enjoyment—Simply enjoying the processes and activities involved in learning is an often overlooked factor in effective learning. A positive attitude inevitably leads to learning success.

Personal Judgement of Need Satisfaction

Older students can be encouraged to think of each of their learning needs as a box, as seen in Glasser's model. Each student can make their own graphic representation of their needs. If the need is being met to their satisfaction in the classroom, the box drawn would be large and well proportioned. If, on the other hand, the student feels that the need is not being met, the box drawn would be small. In such a way, an image can be drawn of the four boxes and their proportional sizes for each student. A student who feels that they are given quite a bit of choice but no real power to make decisions that matter, who feels that they have friends and belong to the community but that there is not much fun at school, might have a model that looks like this:

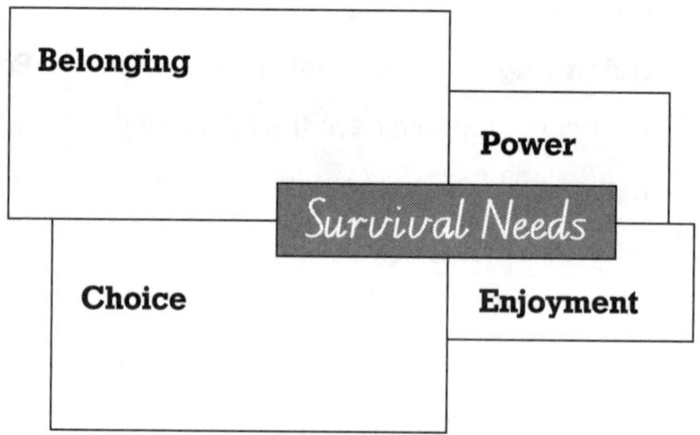

A student who feels that school is a lot of fun, that they belong to a strong group of friends, but that they have little choice in their learning activities and are powerless to involve themselves in curriculum decisions, might have a model resembling the following:

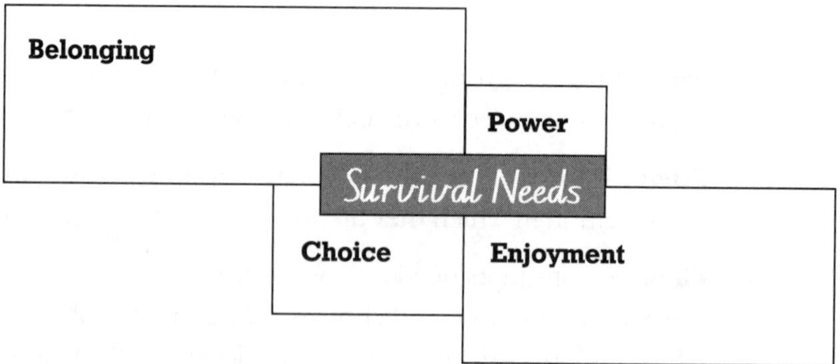

Combining the judgements of individuals into a class picture can illustrate the areas on which teachers need to focus to ensure the learning community is functioning effectively. Individuals give a numerical score for each of the four areas. For example a student may feel that their need for Belonging is being met to a level of 75 per cent.

The scores for all class members for that category are then combined and averaged. In this way, a teacher may discover that there is only one area that the students perceive as inadequate. Activities and strategies to address that particular area can then be implemented.

Strategies for Meeting Learners' Needs

Belonging

- Instigate a Student of the Week guest spot in which students have time to present autobiographical information to others in the class.
- Make cooperative group activities a regular and ongoing part of the class program.
- Develop a class constitution or charter. These processes formalize the ethos and norms of the group.
- Hold regular class meetings with shared leadership roles.
- Use buddy activities within the class or with another class.

Power

- Use a democratic system for determining class monitors in which candidates present a résumé and are voted into office by their peers.
- Create leadership roles within the class community, such as chairing class meetings.
- Instigate school community roles within the classroom, such as Energy Conservation Monitors.
- Implement School Council representation.
- Develop an inquiry approach to curriculum development in which students have input to areas of study.

Choice

- Produce a unit of work or a class project based on the negotiated curriculum model. Activities and specific aspects to be researched will have alternatives and options for students.
- Use contract work requirements.
- Offer activity options within a framework of work requirements.
- Provide choice of seating arrangements within given parameters.
- Negotiate membership of activity groups within a given framework.

Enjoyment

- Provide some unstructured time during the week in which students have free choice of activities or for the class to participate in a game.

Sample class constitution:

In our learning community we are all agreed that the following items are vital. We agree to respect this code and are committed to ensuring that it is a central part of every activity in every day.

We, the students of Class 6E, agree to:

1. *Treat every member of our learning community equally and acknowledge that every person has special talents and expertise.*
2. *Show respect to every person who comes into our learning community, be they a teacher, a student, a visitor or a parent.*
3. *Communicate effectively with everyone in our community.*
4. *Respect the belongings of every other student and use them only with permission from the owner.*
5. *Welcome all students into our groups and activities.*

Signed:

Caitlin Meredith Aaron Jeremy Lillian Kate
Kyle Rebecca Richard King Lok Malin Ailu
Marcus Devin Anthony Nikhila Mervyn Stephen
Jonathon Luke Carla Bianca Rachael Francesca

- Select a "class jester" whose responsibility it is to collect a daily/weekly joke or riddle to share.
- Make time for teacher interaction during free student activities.
- Use informal opportunities to share in a fun way with students; for example, creating an item for the school concert.
- Negotiate a shared reward for class achievements.

2 Curriculum Planning and Assessment

Effective teaching and learning requires a planning and assessment cycle that never stops, but is continually revisited and updated to improve student outcomes. In order to plan and develop an appropriate program for students, teachers need to have mechanisms in place through which they can find the starting points of individual students. Good teaching requires an amount of flexibility, but it is essential to ensure students move on from their starting points. This chapter provides some practical assessment and planning strategies to help with this process.

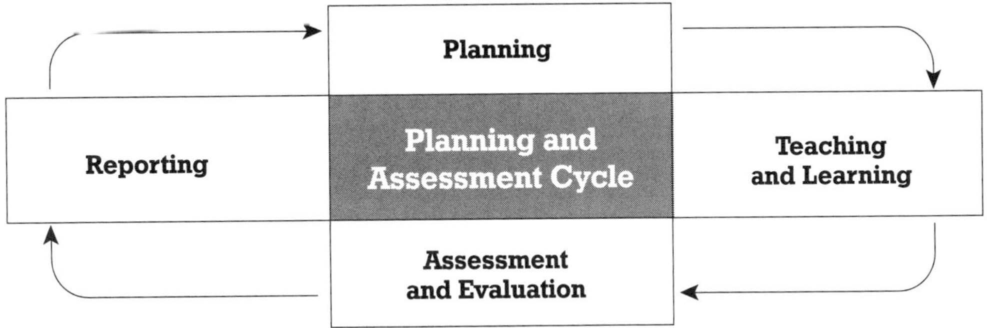

Within curriculum guidelines, each school works in ways that suit its organizational requirements, staff and student population. Planning does require a whole-school approach to ensure consistency throughout the school, as well as to ensure an interesting, child-centred approach with an aim to improve learning outcomes for each student. An integrated studies approach, combining key learning areas, can ensure a more comprehensive curriculum. Social Studies, Science, Technology, and Health and Physical Education are content-based subjects that work well within an integrated curriculum approach. Integrating the process-based subjects of Math, English, the Arts and Languages with other key learning areas makes studies more interesting, relevant and meaningful.

Team Planning

Teams of teachers and administrators can establish planning meetings. Team planning is essential for:

- shared understandings
- efficiency
- consistency across the school
- sharing work loads
- managing the many demands of schools.

Team planning can take the form of one or all of the following:

- **Planning days**—Towards the end of the term, a week is set aside where teams work together on a given day to plan for the coming term. School specialist timetables need to be shuffled so that teachers from a team are released from classroom duties simultaneously.
- **After school sessions**—Staff meetings or team meetings can be set aside or extended to include a planning element. Such sessions can have effective team-building results.
- **Professional development days**—Having a well-planned unit of work ready for a coming school term can provide time to strengthen individual planning.

Regardless of how the planning is managed, it is essential to provide an overview of how the time will be used. The following aspects need to be addressed:

1. Consider:
   - curriculum focus statements
   - key understandings
   - outcomes to be achieved
   - specific content of integrated areas of study.

   Math and English can be monitored by color-coding outcomes to be covered each term.
2. Maintain an overall record of what will be covered for the term.
3. Plan English and Math activities to work in with the integrated unit. Keep a record of focus statements or outcomes to be covered.
4. Plan any other relevant English and Math activities that may be needed for that term.
5. Use term planning to complete weekly or term plans within team units.
6. Regular reflection is essential to make sure gaps in skills and understandings do not occur. By regularly checking off outcomes as they are covered, teachers are able to maintain direction and focus with ongoing week-to-week planning.

Weekly Planning

Teams meeting to plan on a weekly basis are greatly assisted by the use of a planning rubric. A scaffold or planning frame can be of great assistance to organize day-to-day activities and create a consistent approach across a team. The framework should take into account the needs of the team and the school curriculum. The example opposite can be a useful starting point. Activities and lesson preparation can be shared within a team.

Weekly team planning provides the opportunity to revisit term planners and examine how units of work are progressing. Adjustments can be made to units as necessary.

Strategies for Organization

It is vital to organize and store planning documents. This allows documentation to be readily available for the class teacher, visiting teachers or other staff. The presence of such documentation also ensures accountability.

Practical ideas

- Create a folder in which all plans can be stored. A ringbinder is ideal.
- Use plastic pockets to hold plans in such a way that they can be easily viewed.
- Different colored highlighter pens can be used for color-coding each term's work.
- Commercial storage boxes can be helpful for organizing materials.
- Permanent storage holders are useful for keeping all documentation until needed in future years.

Assessment

Assessment has two primary functions:

1. to assess teaching practices and their effectiveness; and
2. to assess student achievement.

As students develop, the curriculum and its delivery strategies need to change accordingly. Assessment allows for such growth.

Teachers need to evaluate individual and group progress to ensure improved student learning. This may involve changing ideas about group structures; that is, groups should remain fluid so that they can change as required. Whether a class is made up of a single-grade level or a multi-aged group of students, groups should have enough flexibility to take account of individual needs. For example, they may need to be in a particular group for Math, and this may change for English or Social Studies. Groups may also change from one task to another within any subject area.

Records and observations are essential to determine what a student has achieved and how future needs can be met. Furthermore, team meetings offer opportunities to share reflections and generate ideas on how best to meet the needs of students.

Weekly Planner

Date: Wednesday, January 3 **Week beginning:** Monday, January 8

ENGLISH

Reading:

Wonderful Camera—comprehension sheet

Rotation: 1. Design camera to take wide-angle photos. 2. Computer activity—use the drawing function to draw a common camera. 3. Teacher activity—text schema activity: functions of the eye. 4. Independent comprehension activity—cloze exercise: functions of human eye.

Writing:

Light and sound reports. Common contractions used.

Continue working on narrative work.

Speaking And Listening:

Production rehearsals. Presentation of evaluation of design of light project.

MATHEMATICS

Number:

Place value to millions.

Table and number fact reinforcement.

Multiplication by two digit multiplier.

Measurement:

Area and perimeter of regular shapes.

Chance and Data:

Tally chart of different lighting in homes.

Space and Shape:

REASONING AND STRATEGIES

In small groups, have students complete activities from *InfoTasks* by Carol Koechlin and Sandi Zwaan, "Considering Alternatives" p. 51 and "Developing a Point of View" p. 68. Discuss the alternatives and opinions formed by students. Examine the strategies used by different groups. Create a list of strategies for the classroom.

INTEGRATED STUDIES

Light and sound—second project to be completed in pairs. Following design brief, build, test, evaluate and modify.

HOMEWORK

Poetry—writing ten lines of rhyming couplets following class activities.

PHYSICAL EDUCATION

Platoon system; hockey, basketball drills, soccer. Interschool sport.

SPECIAL EVENTS

Tournament of Minds—children's performances all day Thursday.

Practical Ways of Recording Ongoing Assessment

The following practical strategies can assist in maintaining teacher observations of student learning.

- **Class lists**
  Copies of class lists can be used to keep ongoing records. Attaching the lists to a clipboard means that they are easy to access during regular class activities.
- **Commercially produced assessment books**
  Page layout in these books is designed to keep records clearly and to access them quickly and efficiently. This can have the added advantage of enabling a team to pre-plan and record common assessment tasks, ensuring consistency and accountability. Some formats allow for recording whole-class at-a-glance checklists as well as individual descriptive comments.
- **Commercially produced reference materials**
  Curriculum support documents produced by government and publishing houses can provide useful resources. Some publications provide indicators for monitoring the learning development of students.
- **Computer software programs**
  Spreadsheet programs allow for efficient numerical records. Descriptive comments can be added using comment boxes. Programs such as these have many features allowing for streamlining of collection, recording and graphic representation of data.
- **Focus assessment group**
  Selecting a small group of students on which to focus for a session/day/week enables detailed and appropriate records of students.
- **Focus assessment task**
  Selecting a specific learning activity to become a focus for data collection can provide broad information about student achievement as well as a specific indication of the effectiveness of a particular task.
- **Peer assessment**
  Learning is a social event. Through personal interactions students obtain valuable feedback on how effective their communications have been. Providing feedback for others can itself be an effective reflective strategy. For the vast majority of students, the opinions and judgements of their peers are powerful learning tools.
- **Ringbinders**
  Removable pages in a ringbinder enable teachers to customize pages for individual students, subject areas or topics. Use of tabs on the pages allows for quick access.
- **Sticky labels**
  Using sticky notes labelled with each student's name and the date can be a practical and efficient way of collecting anecdotal records. Placing these on a clipboard at the beginning of each week enables easy access in the classroom.
  It is appropriate to aim to record something for each student each week to ensure no student is overlooked. These can be quickly transferred to a record book.

Student self-evaluation

Self-evaluation strategies allow students to participate fully and independently in the reflective nature of learning. Responsible learners need to be taught strategies to enable them to become independent in their judgements of their own work. See chapter 4 for more information on self-evaluation strategies.

Possible assessment tools:

	Formal	Informal	Conducted by teacher	Conducted by self	Conducted by peers
Anecdotal notes		✔	✔		
Annotated work samples	✔		✔	✔	
Checklists	✔		✔	✔	✔
Class lists		✔	✔		
Expert group feedback	✔				✔
Portfolios	✔		✔	✔	
Journals	✔	✔	✔	✔	
Performance	✔			✔	
Evaluation sheets	✔		✔	✔	✔
Quizzes	✔	✔	✔		✔
Research projects	✔		✔	✔	✔
Scrapbooks		✔		✔	
Tape recordings	✔		✔		
Tests	✔		✔		

3 Goal Setting and Reflection

Step 1

Setting a goal

- Choose a curriculum context for the goal
- Choose a time frame
- Record the goal

Step 2

Identifying learning strategies to make the goal happen

Step 3

Making a plan

- Select strategies
- Document the plan

Step 4

Keeping the goal in focus

- Display goal in the classroom
- Identify possible obstacles

Step 5

Revisiting and evaluating the goal

- Oral reflection
- Written reflection

As teachers, the notion of teaching to a predetermined goal is so natural that we tend to assume all learners set their objectives independently. It is important for our students to have their own outcomes foremost in their minds. This chapter is aimed at providing a structure for the ways in which we can take students through the process of setting, monitoring and evaluating goals; see blackline master on page 83. Students need assistance in developing appropriate goals and working within a reasonable time frame to achieve them. In short, we need to make a greater effort to make these processes explicit for our students.

The processes detailed in this chapter are illustrated with a case study of James, a Grade 6 student. For each of the sections in which the students complete a task to develop and monitor their goal, James' example has been added to enable teachers to see a real example of the kind of responses and results a student might offer.

Step 1: Setting a Goal

Choose a Curriculum Context for the Goal

In order to set an individual goal, teachers need to work with students to identify the specific skills and behaviors they perceive to be their strengths and weaknesses. These self-evaluations form the basis of the goal setting.

To question the students about the areas which they see as their strengths is quite often to discover a very different picture from the one we paint for them. A simple questionnaire with a five-point scale is one way to ascertain students' ideas. An example of a student self-evaluation survey covering a variety of curriculum areas is provided as a blackline master on page 84. Each of the areas is broken down into more specific skills. Students circle a number on the five-point scale to indicate their judgement about their performance on that skill.

Keeping this questionnaire on file and completing an identical copy at other times during the year can show some changes in perceptions. It can become a useful assessment tool for the class teacher, showing a change in skill level or self-esteem over a period of time. It can also become evidence of learning progress that allows both student and teacher to celebrate success.

The students tend to look carefully at the results of their self-evaluation questionnaires. Only one specific area is needed for identification in order to create an appropriate and specific goal It may be appropriate for the class teacher to initially narrow the field from which the goal is chosen to ensure it is relevant to the specific classroom program; however, it is important to give the students some element of choice. It needs to be *their* goal, identified by *them*. Some examples of goals showing the range of possibilities are given below.

My goal for Term 1 is to increase the speed and accuracy of my 7 and 8 times tables. (King Lok–Math)

My goal for Term 1 is to improve my personal best time in the 100m sprint by 5 seconds. (Kyle–Phys Ed)

My goal for Term 1 is to have a short conversation with someone in French, without having to think about the required vocabulary. (Francesca–French)

My goal for Term 1 is to have all assignments and projects handed in on or before the due date. (Rebecca–General)

My goal for Term 1 is to increase the range of ways in which my sentences begin. (Richard–English)

My goal for Term 1 is to use creative ideas to help raise $100 for our class social service project. (Lillian –General)

Students need to be reminded that goals can come from many different areas of the curriculum, as well as from individual personal needs.

It is important to ensure each goal will be achievable. Initially, students need to work closely with teachers to ensure that goals are set in the context of the class program and also that they are set within the bounds of the possible. Students need to consider the amount of time they will have available to bring about their desired result.

Choose a Time Frame

Students need to have a time frame in which to achieve the goal and there needs to be a clear understanding about when the goal is to be monitored and when it will be evaluated.

Setting a goal for a two-month term is an achievable time frame to begin with. A goal set for the year is difficult to keep focused in the learner's mind and requires the powers of a crystal ball to know, ten months in advance, what is going to be a realistic expectation. A weekly goal, on the other hand, comes around far too quickly!

By starting with a two-month term goal, students are given ample opportunities to reflect on the goal and possibly make modifications if deemed necessary. It is also a good way to organize the goals. Teachers can plan structured activities at the beginning of each term, allowing students to reflect on the progress made in the previous term and moving on to setting a goal for the coming term.

Step 1

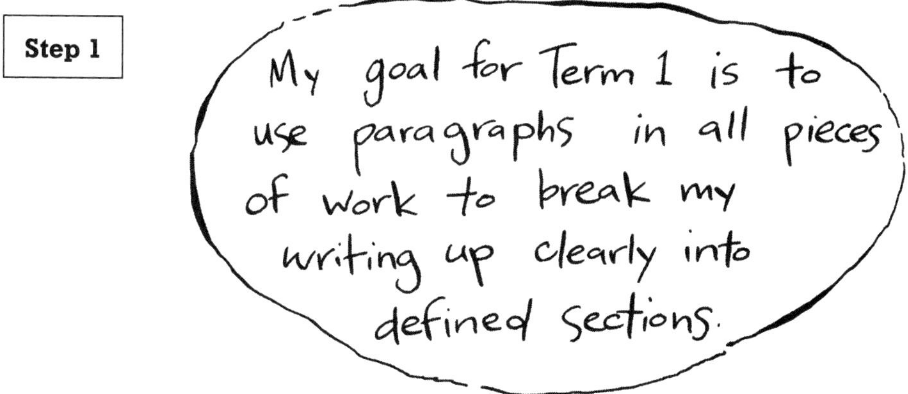

Record the Goal

We can often fall into the trap of assuming students are able to express their goal in appropriate language. To ask a student, "What is your goal for this term?" is to risk a response such as "Math." Time needs to be taken to guide students through the procedure of refining the goal and expressing it in measurable terms. ("If the stated goal is *Math*, how do you know if you have achieved that goal at the end of the stated period?")

Using a framework within which to express the goal is a helpful tool for many students. Instead of being faced with the daunting task of creating a goal out of nothing, they are asked to fill in the blanks with their own choice of details. This can be particularly helpful for ESL or at-risk students.

The goal statement needs a time frame and a curriculum or behavior target. It also needs to be couched in terms of action. In the example shown here, the time frame is "Term 1," the action is to "increase speed and accuracy" and the curriculum area is "times tables."

My goal for TERM 1 is to INCREASE the speed and accuracy of my 7, 8 and 9 TIMES TABLES.

There is also an excellent opportunity here for the class teacher to model a goal on the board or using an overhead projector. This can be done by the teacher setting herself a term goal and going through the steps of publishing this goal in front of the students, or alternatively the class as a whole may choose to set a cooperative class goal. In either scenario, the teacher is able to talk her way through the written part of the task, providing support for students who may need it.

Step 2: Identifying Learning Strategies to Make the Goal Happen

If a goal is set but no guidance provided to make it happen, the chances are that the goal will get no further than being written down on a piece of paper. Students need to explore possibilities for actions they can take to move towards their goal. They do have many learning strategies on which to draw, but without guidance they may never make the link between everyday actions and the occurrence of learning.

As a class, brainstorm the things the students do in order to learn. Some examples may be helpful and may get them thinking beyond academic learning.

- How did you learn to tie your shoelaces?
- How did you learn to make a sandwich?
- How did you learn to count to 100?
- How did you learn to throw baskets in basketball?

The responses are all behaviors that bring about learning. We learn things by:

- practising/rehearsing
- copying/modelling
- being coached
- listening
- asking questions
- experimenting
- making a plan
- reading/researching
- observing
- making mistakes/risk-taking
- revising/repeating
- piloting
- recording/writing.

To bring about my goal, I am going to try these strategies:

1. I will use a point-form plan for each piece of writing and then try and expand each point into a different paragraph.
2. I will read over each finished piece of writing and try to identify the single main point of the paragraph.
3. I will ask Kate to be my writing buddy to check my paragraphs.
4. I will end every piece of writing by asking myself the question "Can I SEE the paragraphs?"

Building up such a list as a whole class is a valuable group activity and provides a repertoire of strategies that students can apply to their individual goals. They take ownership of the strategies, as well as providing the hard evidence that they have learned many things in many ways. Teachers need to take every opportunity to demonstrate to some students that they have already experienced great success as learners and that formal schoolwork goals are as achievable.

Reminder labels:

Learning strategies can easily be displayed around the classroom. If they are referred to on a regular basis, it reminds students that there are many ways they can go about learning. Posters, reminder labels, etc. around the room become just another resource available to students.

It can also be quite valuable to focus on one or two of these strategies each week. By expecting that a couple of strategies will be used at some time over the week for some task, students are once again drawn explicitly to what they actually DO to be effective learners. They may also try a technique that is not normally within their natural repertoire.

Weekly focus:

Weekly Focus

Some goals are quite difficult to measure because they are of a more attitudinal or behavioral nature. These are often goals that are associated with social skills and it can be valuable for all students to revisit them fairly regularly. Make these goals explicit and common to the whole class, rather than on an individual basis, by establishing a weekly focus. This is a shared class focus rather than a goal, which can be used in lessons across the curriculum and does not need the detailed strategy planning of an individual learning goal. Having one or two of these displayed prominently in the classroom and referred to several times by the teacher can keep students focused on positive social interactions. Quite often, there is a direct correlation between these focus statements and elements of the class code that had been created at the beginning of the year.

Step 3: Making a Plan

Select Strategies

Once a goal is established, the next step is to make a plan of the strategies that will be used to achieve the goal. The students will need four or five different things they can try doing to make their goal a reality.

Choosing appropriate strategies is best achieved by sharing creative ideas. Each student selects one strategy they could use to bring their goal to fruition. Using group-work techniques, they share their strategies with others. By sharing techniques, a list can quickly be developed.

Alternatively, students with similar goals can work together to share ideas for strategies. Working on this part of the task with a partner or in a group can provide necessary support for the students. Cooperative group work almost invariably increases the variety and creativity of the goal plans.

Ideas that can be used in the plan

Practise

- Get Dad to ask me times tables every time the car stops at a red light.
- Write spelling list words three times during the week.

Read

- Make a chart of new vocabulary and stick it to the back of the bathroom door.
- Make a time each week to discuss my novel with Mom.

Many students at first find it difficult to think up a variety of creative ways to make their goals happen. It may need some input from the teacher and whole-class brainstorming to come up with a range of ideas.

Document the Plan

The plan needs to be documented and there are several effective ways of doing this. Using a simple 2D map is one way: A sheet of paper is divided into six.

The first section has the goal, the next four sections have outlines of four strategies that will be used to achieve the goal, and the final section has a jingle or slogan to act as a reminder to keep on task with the goal.

The range of ways to record the students' goals is limited only by imagination.

MY GOAL FOR TERM 1 IS TO IMPROVE THE ATTRACTIVENESS OF MY WORK PRESENTATION.	Borrow a lettering book from the library.	Experiment with different kinds of pens to find one that is easy to use.
Use colored pencils and markers to add finishing touches to each piece of work.	Work more slowly and carefully and watch my posture as I write.	EFFECTIVE COMMUNICATION!

my goal for Term 2 is to use paragraphs in all pieces of work to break my writing up into clearly defined sections.	I will use a dot point plan for each piece of writing and then try and expand each dot point into a different paragraph.	I will read over each finished piece of writing and try to identify the single main point of the paragraph.
I will ask Kate to be my 'writing' buddy to check my paragraphs.	I will end every piece of writing by asking myself the question 'Can I see the paragraphs?'	HOLD IT A MINUTE.... put on the breaks! Can I see those paragraph breaks?

Step 4: Keeping the Goal in Focus

Display Goals in the Classroom

It is easy for the goal and its plan to disappear from sight in the regular events of each day. We need to offer students techniques to keep their goals in the forefront of their minds.

Displaying the goals prominently around the room reinforces ideas and shares ideas and strategies with others. An explanatory statement accompanying the display will also help visitors to the classroom—such as parents—understand the role that goal-setting has in the learning community.

Small goal reminders can also be very helpful to keep students focused. Individual students can invent a secret reminder message for themselves and write or draw it on a piece of paper.

Displaying goals:

Possible locations for displaying goals and reminders:

- Attached to the student's work place
- Stuck on the student's chair in the shape of a jogging shoe as a "memory jogger"
- Placed in view on the student's locker
- Displayed on a central notice board in the room
- Attached to the front cover of a workbook or folder
- Suspended from the ceiling.

Identify Possible Obstacles

There is a need to acknowledge that achieving the goal will require hard work and persistence. Knowing oneself as a learner means being aware of one's limitations, accepting one's faults and being able to identify the obstacles that are likely to impede progress.

What teachers perceive as distractions are not necessarily the same as those identified by students. Carefully structured questioning will enable students to explore and identify situations and objects that can distract them from their work. (A distractor readily identified by most teachers is that of talking among friends during work sessions. Students notice other class distractors such as the color and movement on the computer screensaver.)

Identifying distractors can have two consequences:

- Students recognize that there are things happening to keep them off task and they can actually do something about them; for example, turning the computer screen off rather than having a screensaver running.
- Teachers are able to replace classroom discipline statements with observations about distractors. A comment such as, "Jen, you are supposed to be getting on with your work, not chatting with Liz" can be replaced with, "Jen, didn't you identify chatting as one of your distractors? What can you do about it?" The learner is steered into taking primary responsibility for learning.

Step 5: Revisiting and Evaluating the Goal

Oral Reflection

It is imperative that formal time be made available to revisit the goal, such as ending the day with a few minutes to reflect on the day's activities. This allows students to re-connect with the myriad of tasks and activities that they have done. It demonstrates how much they do achieve during a day at school and it gives them some ammunition when they are faced with the question at home, "What did you do at school today?"

Key questions to guide discussion:

- What have we done?
- Why did we do it?
- What did I learn?
- How did I learn?

Greater analysis of the success of the strategies a student is using to achieve the goal is also helpful to keep students on task. If the goal is set for achievement over a two-month period, it is appropriate to analyze progress once or twice through the term. A line marked on the floor can become a continuum along which students place themselves to indicate the extent to which their goal has been achieved in the given period of time. They are then asked to explain why they have positioned themselves where they have. Comments made by one student may ring true for another and suggest that he or she should reposition himself or herself along the line. Such sharing can help the discouraged students recognize that they have made progress.

Written Reflection

Developing a reflective learning journal is another way students can monitor progress towards their goal. This can be set up in diary format with a regular time set aside for a brief comment relating to learning behaviors, strategies and achievements. Many students find it inherently difficult to create a written reflection. Like any other form of text, it requires explicit instruction and individual guidance from the teacher. The written reflection can be supported with sentence starters such as:

"The strategy that has been most helpful so far is…"

"I could improve my progress towards achieving my goal by…"

"My biggest problem is…"

"I am very pleased with…"

A technique for simplifying this written task is to ask students to create a continuum on which to mark their ongoing achievement. Judgements of progress can be recorded on the continuum and dated to build up a pictorial representation of progress towards goal achievement.

Goal continuum:

How is my goal progressing?

10 October

No progress ———————— X ———————— Fully achieved

James' reflective journal:

I started here — I am here now — I want to be here

It is now halfway through the term and I ask myself, "Am I halfway to my goal?" By flicking back through the pages of my workbooks, I would have to say that there is a clear improvement. The paragraph breaks are obvious in most pieces of writing BUT..... they are not always there. Sometimes I need to put more time into the planning. I find the strategy of expanding a dot point the best way to make paragraphs happen, but it is often a pain to actually do.

The airport - Draft 1.

On Wednesday we went to the airport for our class excursion. We went on a bus and we waited at the front gate. We waited and then the bus came and we hopped in and I sat next to Binny. We finally got there.... After it was time to go we said thankyou to Matthew the guide for everything. Then we went back to School.

↓

The airport. — Draft 2.

First paragraph

- Describe the event. When we went to the airport + why.

Second paragraph

- First thing that happened. The bus ride and arriving at the airport.

…

Fourth paragraph

- Conclusion. Going back to school.

↓

Airport Excursion

Last Tuesday, 2nd of June, our class went on an excursion to the airport. We went there because we were learning about flight in Science.

We waited for the bus at the front gate. It was a very bumpy ride.

…

When it was time to go we said thank you and goodbye to Matthew. We hopped on the bus and returned to school.

4 Student Self-evaluation

Reflection, assessment and evaluation are so closely intertwined that it is often difficult to separate them. It is impossible to consider one without either of the others. They play an integral role in curriculum design and involve a wide range of techniques and strategies.

In an effective learning community, assessment is far more than the responsibility of the teacher. The need to reflect critically on learning is logically followed by the need to assess skills and understandings and evaluate them in light of future curriculum direction. Teachers can reflect on their perceptions of what has been learned by a student, but only the students themselves can truly know the extent to which learning has taken place. Self-evaluation is non-competitive and sends a clear message to the students that we, as teachers, value their opinions.

Encouraging students to take some responsibility for self-evaluation is imperative if the skills of learning are to be fully independent. If a student is reliant on a teacher to tell them where they are up to in the learning process before they move on, progress is sure to be impeded. It follows then that, as a part of the learning program, students need to be explicitly taught skills to allow them to make judgements about their own work. From a mentality of the teacher correcting work, there needs to be a considerable shift to an assessment culture in which the student is the key participant.

By introducing the student into the evaluation process as a participant with a valuable contribution to make, teachers are faced with the challenge of teaching their students the skills and strategies required to make meaningful judgements about their work. It means teaching students to be critical readers of their own work; to ask probing questions of themselves and their work.

This perception of the active learner sits well within the culture of negotiated curriculum, of the student as philosopher and of the idea of learning as a process involving multiple intelligences.

There are a number of ways in which classroom teachers can assist their students in structuring self-evaluation. This chapter identifies some of these strategies and suggests ways in which they can be introduced to the students as a part of the development of an effective learning community in which students take responsibility for their own learning.

Skills Checklists

A checklist is a tool commonly used to break down a task into components to be individually identified within the set task. By involving students in the preparation of these tools, they are involved in explicitly identifying the elements within the task. They work collaboratively to provide a list of characteristics or criteria that call for a judgement: *Is this characteristic evident in the text? Is it totally absent? Is it alluded to but not fully developed?* In this way students are required to ask specific questions about their work and use the results to assist them in moving on through the learning process. An example of a student evaluation checklist, Self-evaluation Checklist for Written Narrative is provided as a blackline master on page 85.

Steps in Developing a Checklist

1. Provide a model of the area to be assessed; for example, a piece of text, a student project, a math problem, etc.
2. Analyze the example and, as a group, decide upon the characteristics that are present (or absent), which indicate that it is a good piece of work.
3. List these characteristics and order them.
4. Determine a judgement scale to be used (see below).
5. Pilot the checklist as a group and make alterations as necessary.
6. In pairs, students use the checklist to analyze a further piece of work. Working with a partner encourages dialogue and increases critical engagement with the task.
7. Produce a final checklist rubric for individual use.

Using a Judgement Scale

There are several different ways in which the judgement can be recorded. Again, students are effective decision-makers if given options from which to choose. Possibilities include:

- a numerical scale of 1 2 3 in which 1= little evidence, 2= some evidence, 3= consistently evident;
- a smiley-face scale in which a down-turned mouth, straight mouth and smiling mouth represent the 3-point scale;

- a percentage score;
- a blank line continuum;
- a score out of 10; and
- a scale of check marks (see page 38).

Piloting the Checklist

It is important to work through a draft of the checklist and pilot it with the students. Faults, gaps, inconsistencies and ambiguities often show up when the designed checklist is applied to a real task. The value of working through this drafting and revision cycle in groups or pairs is that thinking becomes verbalized, and inconsistencies or disagreements lead to high-level dialogue about the task as well as the actual piece of work being analyzed.

Applying the Checklist

The process of analyzing the elements of a piece of work is extremely valuable. The resulting checklist should be seen as a readily available tool to be used repetitively and regularly as a part of the learning process. Consequently, the completed checklist needs to be published in a form that is available to the students. Having a stockpile of photocopied checklists stored in the classroom enables students to access them when it is appropriate.

Self-evaluation Scaffolds

A scaffold, or frame, is a series of sentence starters that give the students a lead-in to analyzing their work, for example: "I am happy with…; I think it could have been better if…; Next time I will…" In other words, the scaffolds take the form of a skeleton that is fleshed out by the student's own ideas and opinions.

Scaffolds are valuable because they reduce the anxiety that many students experience when presented with a blank page. They also provide a valuable guide that can, with repeated use, become a natural part of the students' own evaluation repertoire. An example of a Self-evaluation Guide is provided as a blackline master on page 82.

Sample self-evaluation guide:

Title: *The Traveller's Guide to the Solar System*

Context:

This piece of work was completed because . . . *it was the option I chose out of three possible tasks. It was worth 3 points towards the requirement of 20 points of contract-based activities.*

Task outline:

The task given to me was to . . . *write a travel brochure for a tour of the planets in our solar system.*

Judgements:

I am happy with . . . *my brochure*

because . . . *it looks professional and I used my computer skills well to make it. It had useful information about the planets based on a brochure I had at home. It was fun to mix the facts I knew and my imagination about space travel.*

I think it could have been better if . . . *I started it earlier*

because . . . *I had to rush to finish it at home and some sections were too short.*

Next time I do a task like this I will think more about . . . *what should be left out to fit in a little bit about everything.*

Learning Portfolios

A learning portfolio is a collection of a student's work samples taken over a period of time and stored together in one location. The practice of developing and maintaining a portfolio of samples allows students to become actively involved in self-evaluation. By dating their work samples, students have graphic evidence of how their skills developed over time. These collections can be used for close analysis or comparison to help make development explicit to the student. Mere collection and storage of work samples is not enough. A portfolio is nothing more than a file of written work, and is of little value for its own sake unless analysis of the content is made. Only when teachers, students, or both, explicitly examine the content of the portfolios and make judgements about it does the strategy become truly evaluative.

Learning portfolios development over three samples:

Sept. 6

Once upon a time there was a cat. The end.

Feb. 20

My brother was once bitten by a bee. This was a very bad thing for him . . .

May 30

Bang! It had happened. The moment had come and I was less than prepared.
It was time to consider my plight.

Students' portfolios can be given a high profile within the learning community through:

- weekly time dedicated to revisiting the portfolios, including samples, comparing samples over time and so on;
- presentation times in which students share the contents of their portfolios and talk to the group about their perceptions of their work;
- regular teacher–student conferences based around discussion and joint analysis of the content of the portfolio;
- use of portfolios to guide parent–teacher conference discussions; and
- regular presentation of a Student of the Week whose portfolio is displayed for the class or wider community.

Annotated Work Samples

Taking the trouble to analyze samples chosen for inclusion in the portfolio is valuable. A simple way to do this is by using a framework that is completed by the student and attached to the piece of work being included in the portfolio. This need not be extensive, but is an opportunity for the student to include self-evaluation in the regular repertoire of learning behaviors. For the teacher, such a technique can provide an insight into the opinions and judgements of the student. An example of a student work sample blackline master is provided on page 87.

Work sample:

Name of author: Kate Myers **Date:** 17 April

Title: A letter from the trenches

Context: English learning centre task

This work was chosen for inclusion in my folio because . . .

it is the best piece of writing I've done this year.

It shows that I can . . .

use facts that I have researched in my own imaginative setting.

It shows that I know about . . .

- setting out a letter with the address at the top and using clear descriptions to tell other people what an experience might look and feel like.

Peer Assessment

Students gain further insight into the assessment process when they are involved in providing feedback to others. The principles of self-evaluation remain in place, but there is the added requirement that analytical judgements be clearly communicated to others and that they be prepared to justify the feedback offered. While most students feel comfortable in approaching a teacher for comments about their work, and can be open to criticism (in fact they are usually their own harshest critics) when assessing their own work, providing feedback to one's peers is often the most difficult form of assessment. The peer-assessment process requires guidance and structure to be successful. Using a set framework for specific comment, such as shown in the following example, keeps students to the point and ensures positive, constructive feedback. It focuses the assessment and minimizes the danger of personality differences interfering with the true task.

Sample peer assessment for public speech:

Name: Christopher Ross

Topic: Symbols in the Olympic Games

Assessed by: Rania, Laura and Matthew

Scale: ✓ ✓✓ ✓✓✓

Characteristics of a good speech:

Voice

- Clarity ✓✓
- Volume ✓
- Tone ✓✓

Content

- Appropriateness ✓✓✓
- Interest ✓✓✓

Comment:

We like the information you had and the pictures were good.
It was hard to hear you sometimes. You showed the pictures in front of your face and that made it hard to hear.

Peer Checklist

It is helpful for the whole class to be involved in developing the criteria on which judgement is made. Once the process has been followed (see details for developing checklists earlier in this chapter) and a checklist developed for the task, students form pairs or small groups to complete the assessment. Again, the value of shared work is in the opportunity it provides for dialogue between students. A blackline master Peer Assessment for Public Speech is provided on page 88.

By providing a written summary of the group's judgements, the student being assessed is able to keep a record of the feedback. If several groups have assessed the one piece of work, the student is able to compare judgements and use the information gained in a kind of moderation process.

Expert Groups

Another method of providing peer assessment is to divide the class into "expert" groups. Each group has the responsibility for analyzing one aspect of the student's work and providing detailed feedback on that one aspect. This method allows for students to be more focused in the criticisms they make. Each group provides a written summary of their judgements for the student who is being assessed.

Some of the components being assessed will be generic across tasks. For example, any oral presentation, regardless of the context or content, will require feedback on the effective use of voice.

It is possible to create permanent expert groups, with the specific skills being assessed recorded on laminated cards. This makes the resource a permanent part of the classroom.

Expert group posters:

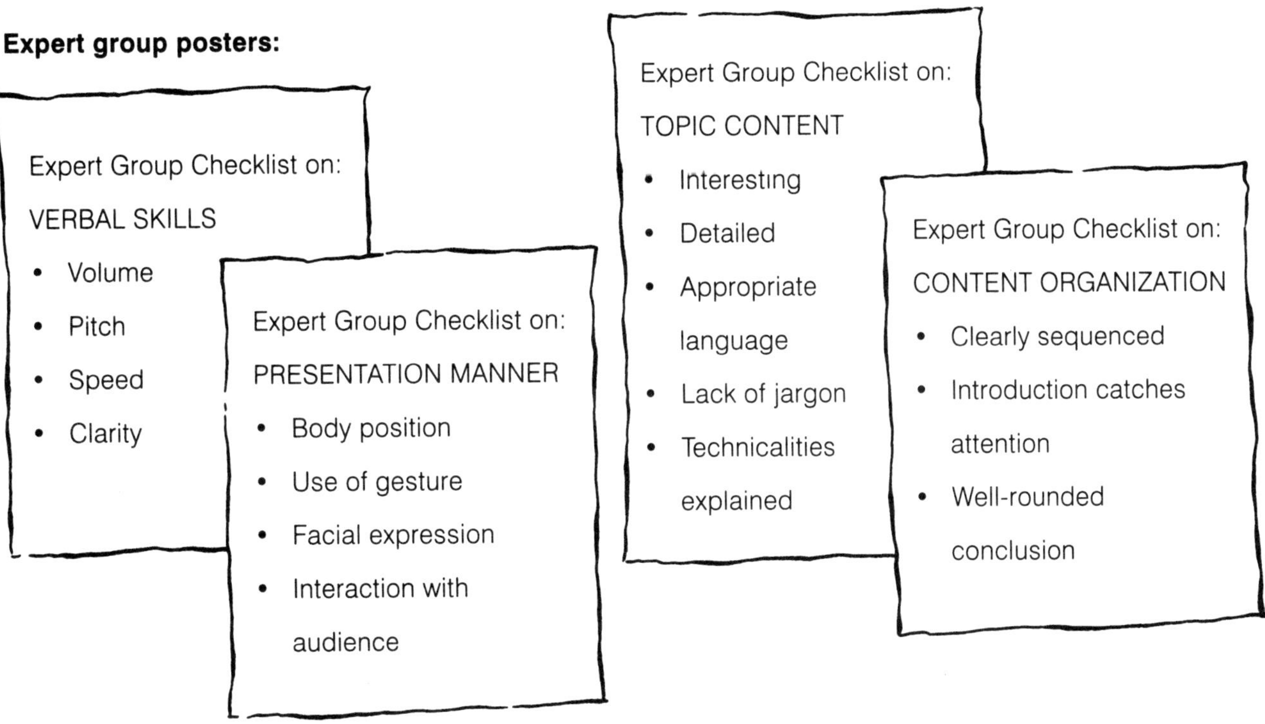

5 Establishing Learning Centres

The Learning Centre approach to teaching is a model that requires careful planning. A teacher cannot divide the class into groups, issue each with a task and then expect all individuals to settle quickly and effectively without clearly briefing students on the following:

- basic rules and responsibilities for all when working in groups
- outline of the task
- expected outcomes from such activity

This model of classroom organization can have many benefits. A great deal of research has been conducted into cooperative or collaborative learning, and the more recent findings are that learning is, indeed, a highly social and interactive process.

Students who engage in activities that have been specifically designed to involve thoughtful dialogue or task sharing are far more likely to use critical or divergent thinking skills. Working collaboratively allows students to consider ideas from a number of different viewpoints. It allows them to explain and develop their own ideas and requires them to be able to justify or modify these ideas as other group members question or expand upon them.

Working with small groups of students is a preferred method of teaching, for a number of reasons:

- Individuals have a higher rate of participation where there is less competition for talking time.
- Specific learning needs can be addressed by working with a more homogenous group of learners.

- More detailed evaluation can be made if there are fewer students to be monitored.
- Groups need to learn independent working skills that are valued, encouraged and necessary to effective management.
- Peer tutoring can become a regular learning strategy.
- Group work encourages and develops a positive and effective learning community within the classroom.

Incorporating learning centres into an ongoing classroom program requires careful planning and consideration of management and curriculum issues. This chapter considers the issues relating to the following:

1. managing the physical environment;
2. monitoring a number of groups simultaneously; and
3. setting appropriate activities for use in the learning centres.

Managing the Physical Environment

Furniture Layout

Although a learning centre style of teaching will not operate all day, it is helpful to have the classroom structured in such a way that movement into groups and the rotation between groups are conducted smoothly. If four groups are to operate, having the tables set up into four clusters allows for easy identification of, and differentiation between, each group.

Possible furniture layout for a class of 30 students:

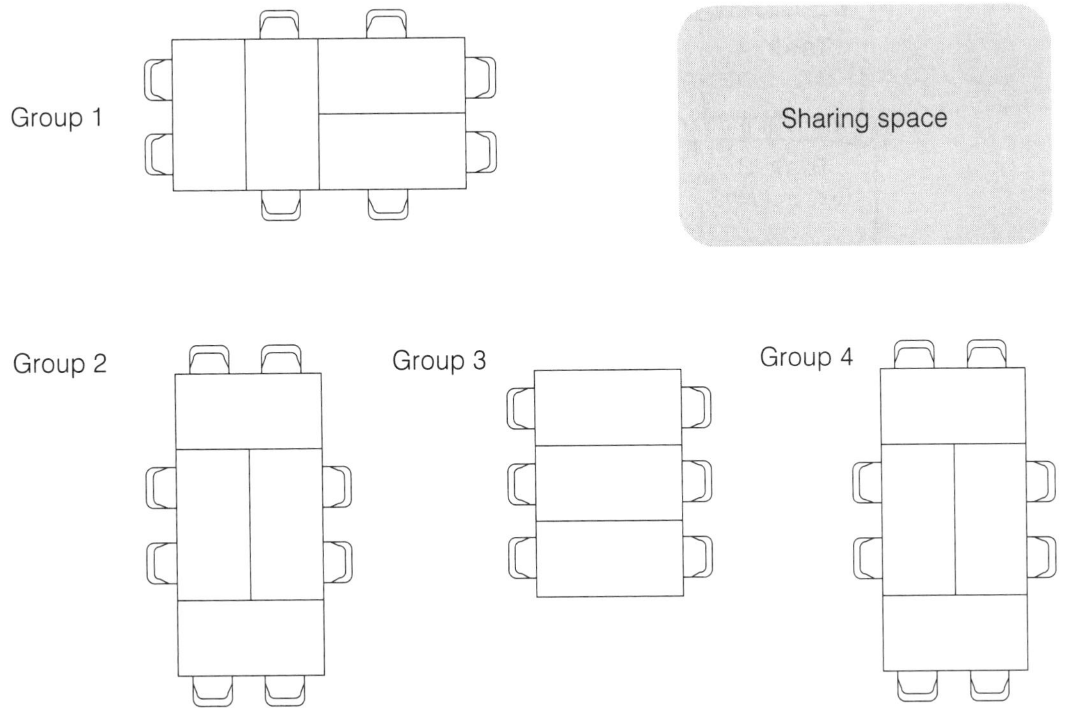

Having the students grouped this way will:

- keep noise to a minimum as students work together or support one another in the tasks;
- enable materials needed by the group to be close to each group member;
- enable a small set of resources to be used on a rotational basis, thus allowing for maximum utilization of minimum materials;
- allow the teacher to monitor the on-task behavior of groups, particularly in terms of monitoring when the group has completed the given activity; and
- enable a parent helper program to be implemented effectively.

The number of groups operating within the classroom will vary according to individual situations. These factors may include:

- class size
- class dynamics
- furniture limitations
- availability of assistance
- range of student needs and abilities
- teacher experience.

As a starting point, working with four groups is manageable and effective.

Storing Activity Requirements

Four groups operating at once means that four sets of equipment may need to be readily available to the students. Some ways of organizing this are suggested below:

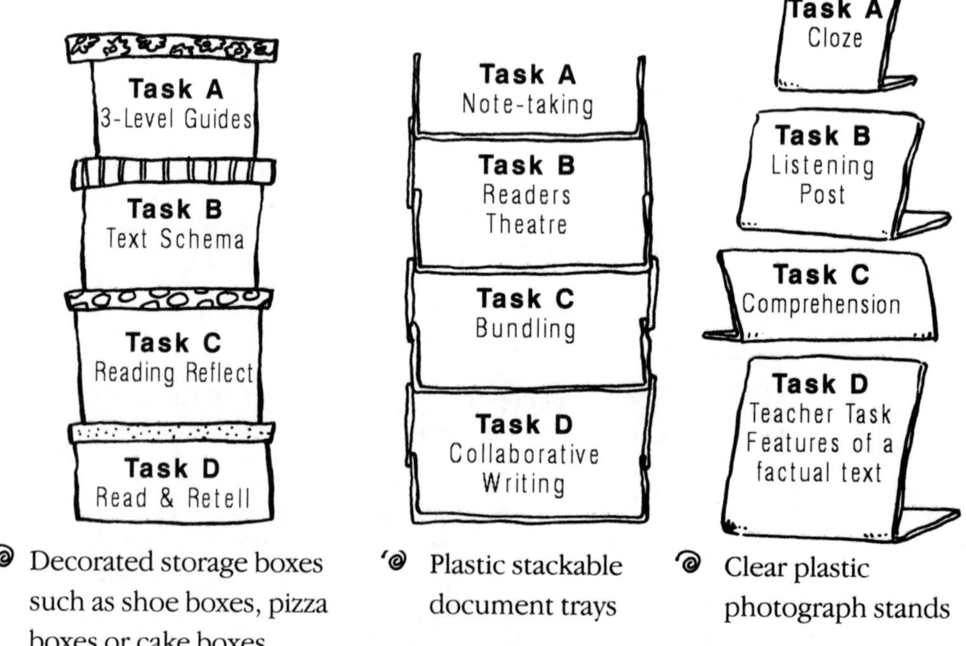

- Decorated storage boxes such as shoe boxes, pizza boxes or cake boxes
- Plastic stackable document trays
- Clear plastic photograph stands

Having tasks presented in such ways allows for simple storage of the materials when rotation groups are not in effect. They simply stack up out of the way in a cupboard or on a shelf.

Organizing the Group Plan

It is important that names of students are clearly displayed around the room to provide a reminder of who is in each group. By making a small chart of each group's membership, the charts can become a part of the organizing plan. It is a good idea to create a group name to distinguish between groups, as it can get very confusing with task numbers, group numbers and table numbers.

Group plan for rotations:

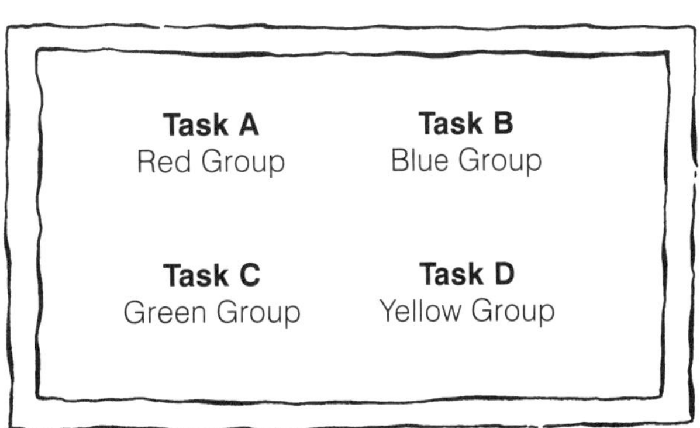

Monitoring Groups at Work

Selecting Group Membership

Criteria used to determine the composition of each group can vary greatly. It is advisable to make membership fluid so that changes can be made to increase the effectiveness of the group.

1. Groups can be of **similar skill level** in the curriculum area being taught.
2. Individuals with the **same specific learning needs** can be brought together for a teaching session to address those particular needs.
3. Groups can be **random.**
4. **Membership can be spread** so that each group has at least one strong leader, one academic struggler etc.
5. Students with the **same learning style** preferences can be grouped together; e.g., visual learners.
6. Students with similar **personality styles** can be grouped. For example, outgoing verbal contributors can be grouped together, while reticent students are kept separate. This can be a useful way of ensuring that quiet students have to participate rather than relying on others to jump in and fill the silences, while at the same time ensuring that dominant contributors have some competition for an audience.
7. There can be value in working with groups where participants are of the **same gender**.
8. Students enjoy having the opportunity to work in **friendship groups**.

Establishing Group Work

Students need to be taught how to work in groups. This means not only working cooperatively as a member of a group, but also being considerate of other groups working in the same room. For a teacher starting off with multiple groups, the key advice is: **Start simple**. There needs to be a build-up of the number of groups operating at once, along with a build-up in the independent working skills required of the groups.

This is a wonderful opportunity for parents or teacher aides to make a real difference in the classroom. It can be very helpful having a second pair of hands to assist by working with another group or moving between groups, keeping students on task and offering assistance where it is needed.

Setting ground rules and training students to work in groups is not difficult. They need to understand that the rights of each individual and group rely on every single class member taking responsibility for their own learning. This is a fundamental understanding within an effective learning community. Students need to know that while working with a group, the teacher is not available for others. This means that the group members need to work together to solve problems or utilize resources within the room.

At some stage during a rotation of activities, the whole class needs to be together to allow opportunities for:
- questions regarding clarification of activities;
- sharing strategies for completing activities;
- feedback from students on level of difficulty and time allocation of activities; and
- reinforcing teacher expectations.

Setting Appropriate Activities

Where to Start

The level of difficulty of tasks being performed by independent groups needs to be carefully considered. Initially, these tasks need to be **straightforward** and **familiar** to the students. Revision of work or other activities requiring little guidance are ideal while students become familiar with the learning centre processes. The tasks can increase in complexity as students become more skilled in group work.

Timing

The learning centre timetable must fit within the existing class timetable. Ideally, this approach should be used each day. However, reality dictates that it will not always be possible. One rotation to be completed within the literacy or numeracy time of each day is achievable and effective; it is not necessary that groups rotate through a number of tasks consecutively on one day.

A daily English program would include aspects of reading, writing, speaking and listening. Literacy and numeracy sessions may be structured as follows:

LITERACY	NUMERACY
• Shared reading	• Automatic response
• Rotational tasks	• Rotational tasks
• Independent reading	• Sharing ideas/strategies
• Sharing completed activities	• Whole-group teaching
• Independent or shared writing	

The amount of time given to each element of the session is dependent on a number of variables. Timetable restrictions, individual class needs and age of students all need to be considered. The time allocated to the group rotation task will need to be gradually built up as skills develop; however, 30 to 40 minutes would be an appropriate time frame to work towards.

Following a rotation task with an independent activity such as quiet reading is an ideal opportunity for the teacher to deal with any necessary correction or to record anecdotal or formal assessment.

Beginning rotational tasks with the whole class working together as a group provides the opportunity to reinforce activity requirements and expectations, as well as allocating groups to follow-up tasks. At the start of a new set of rotation, extra time needs to be allowed for introducing and explaining new activities.

6 Putting the Principles into Practice

Teaching a small group of students rather than the whole class at once has many advantages.

- It enables the teacher to target specific learning tasks at students who need work on those particular aspects.
- It enables individual students to have a greater input to the teaching session.
- It enables the teacher to monitor and assess more closely the extent to which each student has mastered a specific skill.

Managing a classroom to allow for small-group teaching requires careful planning. Having students work independently on a task while the rest of the class works in other learning centres is a skill that takes time and tuition. The teacher cannot assume that individuals will be able to organize themselves into this work environment, as many students will have had little, if any, experience in working independently on a task with a group of others while the teacher is otherwise occupied.

This chapter outlines some of the strategies that can be used for teaching English within this model of rotational group learning centres. It offers guidelines to assist the teacher in establishing the routines and teaching the students the skills and behaviors they will need to use within this learning model. Each strategy is explained and steps in preparation and teaching are provided. Working examples are provided in many cases. The strategy must be explicitly taught to the students and then they can use it independently while the teacher is working with another group.

An outline of each task and steps required to complete the task are provided for students. These pages may be copied and displayed for the students to access. In each case, the broad task outline will need to be supplemented with the specific text chosen by the teacher.

Note: Because students are working on a range of different activities and most cannot access the teacher once the activities have begun, the teacher must have all resources and equipment that the students are likely to need close at hand.

Getting Started

Teaching Students to Work in an Independent Group

In this rotation model, the teacher focuses on one small group only. Students in the other groups need to have the following guidelines clearly established:

1. The teacher cannot be approached by a member of any group other than the one with which the teacher is working.
2. Students needing assistance must access the other students in their own group for help.
3. Students must work quietly to allow the others to focus on their different tasks.
4. Students must work in a cluster with others involved in the same task.

Structuring the Time Block

A simple sequence of events is helpful for structuring the block of time that has been allocated for such rotational group tasks.

1. A whole-class meeting is a good way to focus students' attention on a specific skill or concept that may be underlying all the learning centre tasks. For example, if the teacher is introducing a specific text style, a short whole-group discussion of such an example can be helpful in focusing student attention.
2. The teacher will need to remind students about which group is attending to which task. Some tasks will need a recap to remind students about what is required from the task. Quickly running through individual activities in such a way allows students to ask questions to clarify their understandings. It also allows the teacher to make specific reference to any tasks that have been causing difficulties and to restate instructions.
3. The learning centre tasks need to be allocated a certain time. The length of time can be increased as students become familiar with the organization. Initially, 20 minutes of on-task time is enough. Different student groups will have different concentration abilities, but usually 30–40 minutes is adequate for independent work.

4. Following the group tasks with a whole-class independent silent reading session of approximately 20 minutes allows the teacher time to compile records and check work. The learning centre tasks require the students to complete written work which must be checked on a regular basis, or correction can build up to unmanageable levels. By using a short time after the tasks have been completed, the teacher is able to keep on top of the correction and provide immediate feedback. This time is also helpful for the teacher to extend upon evaluation notes made for the target group during the rotation task time.
5. Providing a time at the end of the session for individuals to share their work can have several benefits. It allows students to use work completed by others as a model or example when they are rostered to complete that task. In this way it can clarify instructions for some students who may need it. It can also act as a time for the teacher to make a teaching point based on some element of the example shown to the class. Many students value the opportunity to give their work a wider audience than just themselves and the teacher. This is not always the case, but as presentation of work becomes a regular and expected part of the learning process, students pay greater attention to the needs of their audience when they are undertaking the task.

Keeping Assessment Records

Working with a small group of students allows excellent opportunity for detailed record-keeping. There are a number of ways in which records can be kept. Chapter 2 provides strategies that can be implemented in this model.

Strategies for Teaching English

Each of the following strategies can be used as a teacher-led task with detailed questioning focusing on a teaching point. Once students have used a strategy in this supportive structure, they can revisit it in a learning centre setting. They should be confident to attempt the task without teacher leadership but with the support of their peers.

The student activity instruction sheets are designed so that they can be photocopied, laminated and stored within the learning centre for access by groups at the point of need.

Text Schema—Whole-text Context

Text schema is a jigsaw-style task in which the student assembles pieces of a written text to create a sensible whole.

The teacher selects a text that is suited to the topic being studied. The students use their knowledge of text features and content flow to piece together the text that has been cut apart and jumbled by the teacher. This strategy can be used with a range of different text styles and is particularly useful for highlighting the features of different styles that identify them as belonging to one style or another.

Purpose

Text schema is a strategy that helps students identify the features of text. A variety of text types can be used, but it is particularly useful when working from a factual text model. It guides students through the organizational features of factual text and makes explicit the model from which students can generate their own text.

Steps in Preparation

1. Find an example of the text type to be studied. (Student magazine articles are particularly useful.)
2. Photocopy the article.
3. Cut the text into discreet sections—heading, illustrations, captions, separate paragraphs, subheadings, diagrams, etc.
4. Paste sections onto one sheet, mixing them up.
5. Photocopy the mixed-up text for each child or each group (as required).

Variations:

- Prose text can be copied and cut into distinct paragraphs.
- Cut text pieces can be collected in an envelope for jigsaw-style recreation by individuals or groups.

Steps in Teaching

1. Show students the jumbled pieces of text and ask them to consider the ways in which pieces are different.
2. Ask them if they can identify any of the pieces as having a specific job to do in communicating information. (The heading in large font will be obvious.)
3. Ask students to consider the sections of text they would expect in such a piece of writing; for example, columns of text mixed with illustrations.
4. Identify and match up parts of the jumbled text that belong together.
5. Ask students to consider which paragraph of text might be the first of the article. What are the clues within the text that make it clearly an introductory paragraph?
6. Students try to order paragraphs according to meaning flow. Some students will find specific references to the subject that give clear indication of order.
7. Ask students to consider the best locations within the text for illustrations, captions, diagrams, etc.

Text Schema—Whole-text Context

Student Instructions

The Task

In this task you will be required to look carefully at sections of text, then put them together so that they flow properly and make sense. Use the knowledge that you already have about text. Think about:

- the size of the font;
- the way the words are put on the paper;
- the meaning of the words; and
- how the pieces are linked to make the text flow.

Procedure

1. Cut the sections of text away from one another.
2. Read each section of text.
3. Organize the sections into a sensible order so that the meaning flows. Look for the clues mentioned above.
4. Arrange headings, graphics, etc. in places that you think would make sense within the body of the text.
5. Paste the sections into their final arrangement.

Text Schema—Sentence-level Context

For this text schema task, students are given a selection of words prior to reading an expository piece of text. After introducing the topic, they use their words to create sentences which they might expect to find in the text. The sentences are then shared, discussed and compared. Students read the text and confirm their predictions, again sharing their findings.

Purpose

The purpose of this task is to determine students' ability to make predictions and then to confirm these. It also enables teachers to check concept and vocabulary development, along with students' ability to state a point of view. This activity provides a wealth of information regarding general comprehension of text.

Steps in Preparation

1. Select a piece of text appropriate to student reading levels and curriculum content.
2. Select three key sentences from the text.
3. Copy the sentences onto an index card and cut up the words.
4. Place the mixed up words from the three sentences into an envelope. Note: An envelope will be needed for each student, so multiple copies of the sentences will be required.

Steps in Teaching

1. Tell the students they have a number of words in their envelope that need sorting into sensible sentences.
2. Discuss strategies students may use to create sentences. These could include noting punctuation conventions, student general knowledge, and semantics (does the sentence make sense?).
3. Students independently create sentences using all available words.
4. Compare sentences and predict what the original text might be about.

5. Students read the text and confirm their predictions, looking at the overall text and its argument. Discussion resulting from this will enable students to strengthen their ideas regarding the topic.
6. By this stage, students will be forming their own point of view about the issue. This needs to be discussed and expanded to identify main points and supporting arguments. These main points can be used to create a spoken or written text demonstrating understanding of expository text.

Sample: Carnivorous plants

Sentence 1: The small plants on the ground usually catch crawling insects.

usually	plants	insects.	on	The
ground	crawling	small	the	catch

Sentence 2: Carnivorous plants come in many different shapes and sizes, depending on what they are trying to trap.

and	sizes,	what	Carnivorous	trying
depending	different	plants	are	to
come	many	they	trap.	in
shapes	on			

Sentence 3: They are called sundews because the droplets of sticky liquid on the end of the tentacles glisten like dew in the sunlight.

droplets	the	tentacles	because	They
sunlight.	called	glisten	are	on
the	of	sticky	end	like
sundews	liquid	the	of	dew
in	the			

Text Schema–Sentence-level Context

Student Instructions

The Task

You will be given an envelope containing three sentences that are cut up into separate words. The words fit together to make three sentences about a text. While you are moving your words around to make sentences, consider what the text might be about and the argument it is presenting.

Procedure

1. Independently, remove the words from the envelope and sort them to make three sentences. All words should be used.
2. Move the words around to try out different combinations.
3. Read your sentences aloud. Do they make sense? Is the punctuation correct?
4. Compare your sentences with those of another member of your group. Together, discuss what you think the original text from which the sentences were taken might be about.
5. Discuss your ideas as a group.
6. Read the original text. Find the matching sentences and compare them with yours. Were your ideas accurate?
7. As a group, determine what point of view is presented in the text. Do you agree or disagree with the author's point of view? Why/Why not?
8. Be prepared to present your ideas and reasons for your opinion to other students.

Concept Mapping

Concept mapping is a strategy that requires students to identify key concepts and consider the relationships between them. It provides a framework in which students develop a graphic or pictorial representation of the key concepts outlined in a text.

Purpose

Concept mapping can help students organize their thoughts and knowledge about a given topic. It can assist with reading comprehension and is applicable to a range of disciplines. Concept mapping encourages divergent and reflective thinking, and focuses student attention on the identifying and labelling relationships between key concepts. As well as providing a mechanism through which students can present their knowledge, it is an invaluable diagnostic tool for teachers.

Steps in Preparation

1. Select the text to be used for the mapping task.
2. Decide which concept labels from the text will be provided for the students.
3. Make the map starter on individual sheets or on a master for students to copy. Alternatively, use the blackline master provided on page 89.
4. Provide a set of appropriate relationship labels for use on linkages.

Steps in Teaching

1. Read through the text with the students.
2. Ask students to select a topic word that would be appropriate for the hub of the graphic wheel. In other words, what is the text about?
3. Discuss the key concepts that are outlined in the text. Place each concept in a box around the topic box.
4. Ask students what relationship each concept has to the topic. Try to come up with labels to put on the linkages.
5. Determine if the concepts have linkages to one another. Join with lines and add labels.
6. Ask students to provide more information from the text. As a group, decide whether this new information can be presented graphically using more boxes and links.

Sample concept map:

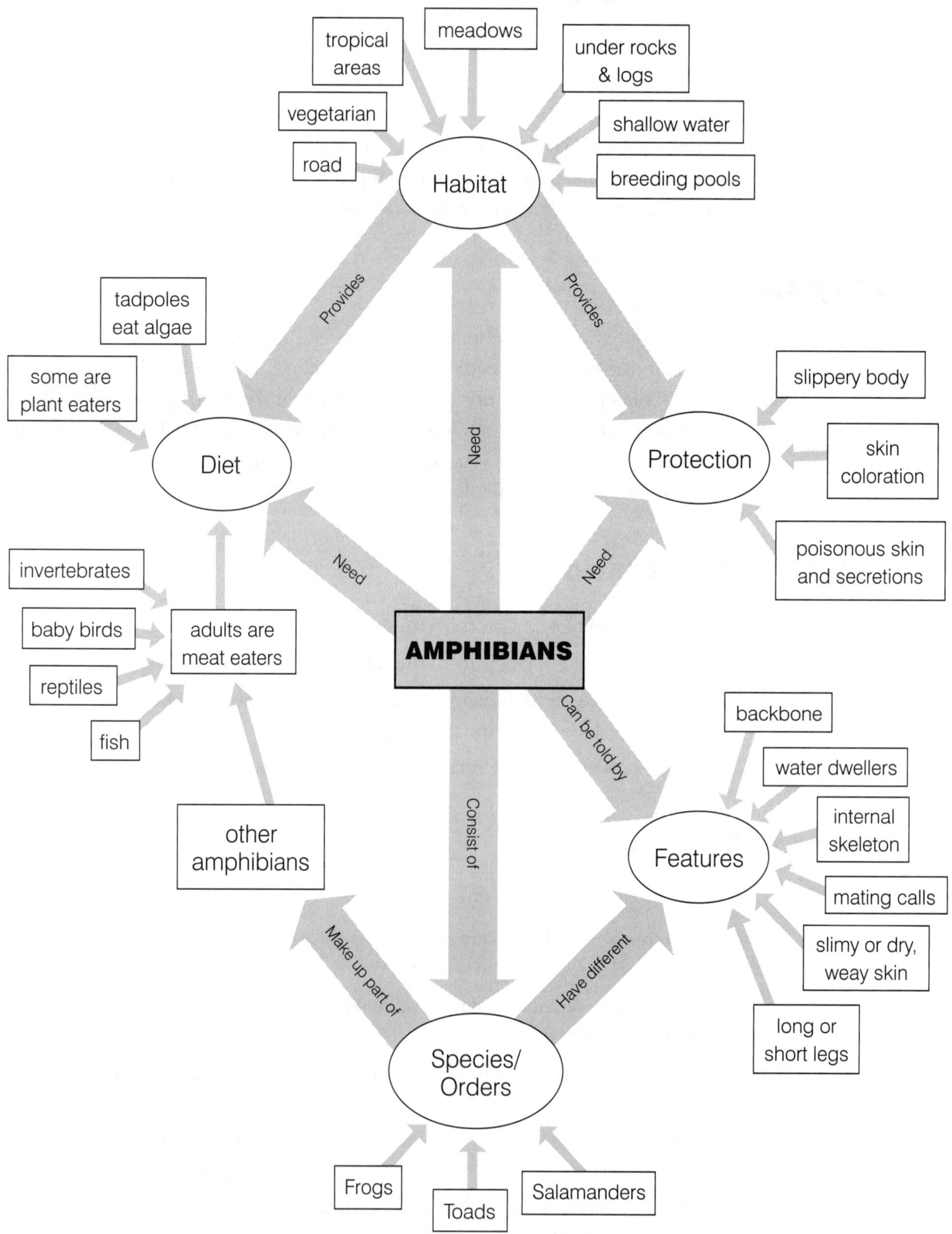

Concept Mapping

Student Instructions

The Task

You will be required to read a piece of text and then present the key information in a pictorial format. You will need to think about the main points provided in the text and decide how they are related.

Procedure

1 Read through the text carefully, at least once.

2 Choose a title or topic word that suits the text. In other words, what is the text about? Write your title in the centre box.

3 Select four or five key words that sum up the main concepts or ideas discussed in the text. Write these in the circles surrounding the title box.

4 Choose words or phrases that could be used to label the lines that join the concepts to the topic. Write the labels along the lines.

5 Consider whether additional lines need to be drawn in to link the concepts to each other. Draw them in, if appropriate, and label them.

6 Extend the concept map with other words to show further ideas presented in the text. Include linking lines and labels as before.

Data Charts

A data chart is a grid on which information about one topic is recorded and organized into a structure. This information can then be used to produce a written report. Notes are collected from a number of different resources and set down in a pre-arranged format to enable comparison across references.

Purpose

Data charts can be used as a scaffolding on which students organize information from a number of different sources. In this way, it supports note-taking skills by providing a structure. Data charts enable all students to organize information clearly and are particularly helpful for students who have difficulty organizing information into a workable format. It reinforces the need for information to come from more than one source. This strategy is a tangible way in which students can compare the ways in which different sources present a single piece of information. Different kinds of texts, including oral and pictorial references, can be brought together for comparison and contrast.

Steps in Preparation

1. Select the topic to be researched by students.
2. Select three or four references to be accessed by students. Clearly, the age, experience and expertise of students will determine the number and complexity of resources selected.
3. Determine five or six headings under which information can be organized. Again, the complexity of these headings will vary according to the student group. It may be appropriate for students to devise their own headings.
4. Place references and headings onto a grid to be completed by students. This might be done on an individual, group or whole-class basis, depending on the teacher's specific purpose. Introducing students to this strategy will require a group or whole-class example to be used as a model. A Data Chart blackline master is provided on page 90.

Steps in Teaching

1. Introduce the topic to the students and ask what they already know about it. Record information provided by students.
2. Ask students about resources that might be useful in finding out more about the topic. Investigate the collection of these, if not already at hand in the classroom.

3. Select the required resources and record the reference details for each one down the left-hand column of the data chart.
4. Ask students to suggest headings that might be helpful to categorize information once it is located in the resources.
5. Use this information to create five or six headings to be researched. Place each heading in a heading box in the top row of the data chart.
6. Skim read the first reference to locate any information that might be recorded under one of the headings. These do not have to be in sequential order. Note the information as it is located.
7. Repeat this process with each of the other resources.
8. When all resources have been used, the information recorded in each column can be collated and written in full sentences to create a paragraph. This step is the move from note-taking to creating the report. (See the outline given for Bundling.)

Sample data chart:

Name: .... **Topic:** ENERGY

	Question A: What is energy?	Question B: Where is energy found?	Question C: How is energy used?
What we already know:	• Electricity • Is a force • Is renewable e.g. solar • Is non-renewable e.g. fossil fuels	• Is formed in different ways • Burning fossil fuels • Sun • In atoms – nuclear	• Lighting • Essential to our lives • Can be overused
Resource 1: Hipgrave, J. & Thomas, R, Energy, Macmillan, Melbourne, 1991	• Moving water	• Trees store energy which is released by burning • Food provides humans with energy • Wind	• Makes things move • Powers machines • Most power used for heating & cooling
Resource 2: Lambert, M, Energy Technology, Wayland, Hove, 1991	• Light – solar • Heat • Water – hydro • Coal & oil – fossil fuels • Nuclear • Movement – kinetic	• Sun gives heat and light • It is everywhere	• Is not going to run out soon • Developed countries use by far the most energy

Data Charts

Student Instructions

The Task

This activity provides a framework for making notes about a topic. It will help you collect information and organize it into appropriate sections. It requires you to use a range of resources to find information and record carefully the publication details of these resources.

Procedure

1 Record the topic you are researching at the top of your chart.

2 Record publication details of the resources you have selected down the left-hand column on the data chart grid.

3 Select five or six areas of the topic that you want to find out more about.

4 Record these headings in the Heading boxes along the top row of the data chart grid.

5 Scan one resource for information that relates to any of the headings you've selected. Note any information you find in that resource under the appropriate heading in that row.

6 Repeat this procedure with the other resources.
Note: You may have blank boxes in cases where the resource does not provide information about one of your headings.

Note-taking

Note-taking is a strategy appropriate to all curriculum areas. It is a strategy in which students identify the main points and supporting evidence in a given text. A variety of texts can be used for this purpose, including fiction, factual and spoken versions.

Purpose

Note-taking can be used to assist students in the development of accurately identifying key words, ideas and information presented in text, and in organizing and sorting their information. The skill of note-taking has wide application in any learning context; providing students with explicit instruction, modelling and practice at a young age will enable them to develop these vital skills for future learning. This activity can be extended to developing summarizing skills.

Steps in Preparation

1. Select a simple text appropriate to the current learning context or integrated unit. As this is a step-by-step process it is advisable to start with a short text. A text divided into four paragraphs will usually provide four subsections that students can identify.
2. The teacher may choose to develop a scaffold to enable students to fill gaps in a prepared table rather than working without guidance. Examples are given below, and a note-taking blackline master is provided on page 91.

Note: It is essential for the teacher to be familiar with the text to effectively demonstrate note-taking skills.

Steps in Teaching

1. Tune students into the piece of text before reading by using title, diagrams, illustrations and headings to discuss what they might expect to find. This provides students with the opportunity to bring their prior knowledge to the text.
2. Identify what the piece is about. (This will almost invariably be in the title.) Students should be able to identify possible sections within the text that will add detail to the title.
3. Ask students to read the first paragraph independently and then discuss as a group what they believe is the key word or phrase in the paragraph.

4. Students record the word or phrase in the selected scaffold.
5. Students read the next paragraph, finding supporting evidence for what they have just read or identifying new ideas that may have been presented.
6. They again record key words or phrases, either as a second heading or as a subsection for the previous recording.
7. Steps 3 to 6 are repeated to the end of the text.

Sample note-taking scaffolds:

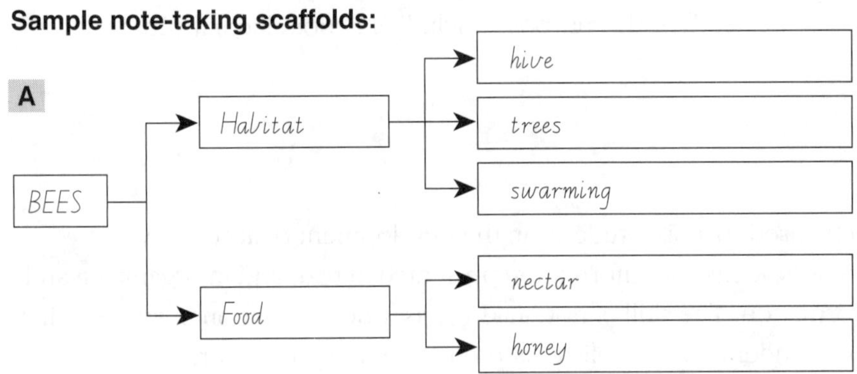

B **Topic:** BEES **Name:** Sean McCourt **Date:** July

Habitat	Gathering Food
Food Production	Finding Direction

C

Name:
Topic: THE SOLAR SYSTEM

Subheading	Details
THE SUN	Detail 1: Strong force of gravity keeps planets in orbit.
	Detail 2: Huge ball of super-hot gas.
	Detail 3: So hot it heats and lights all planets.
INNER PLANETS	Detail 1: four inner planets are: Mercury, Venus, Earth and Mars.
	Detail 2: Have hard rocky surfaces suitable for spaceship landings.
	Detail 3: Earth is the only planet with life-sustaining water
OUTER PLANETS	Detail 1: five outer planets are: Jupiter, Saturn, Uranus, Neptune, Pluto.
	Detail 2: All but Pluto are giant planets with icy surfaces.
	Detail 3: All have natural satellites, from Pluto which has one to □ Saturn which has more than 17

Note-taking

Student Instructions

The Task

This activity gives you a framework for making notes found in a text. You will be required to record your information and organize it into sections.

Procedure

1 Skim the text to look for a title, headings, illustrations or diagrams that tell you what the piece is about.

2 Discuss in your group what the main heading of the text is and record it on your grid.

3 The group will need to decide on suitable headings for the subsections on your grid. When discussing the text, think about important information that might fit into the headings.

4 Read the first paragraph by yourself, thinking about what words or phrases might tell you the main idea. Do the same with the remaining paragraphs.

5 As a group, discuss your ideas and record the key words or phrases in your grid under the correct subheadings.

Read and Retell

Read and retell is a simple strategy in which a student reads a set piece of text and retells it in some way. Incorporating key word identification into the process requires the student to identify the word or phrase that encapsulates the main idea of the paragraph. When completed in a teacher-led group, the task is an oral one. When students have been through the process with teacher guidance, they can complete the task either by writing their responses individually or by working orally with a partner.

Purpose

Retelling a piece of text allows a student to clearly communicate their level of comprehension. It allows the student to clarify the main content of the text and sort out the sequence, main points and important details. Identifying the key word or phrase in a section of text is a form of simple summarizing, and assists greatly with written summaries and report-writing.

Steps in Preparation

1. Select a piece of text appropriate to student reading levels and curriculum content.
2. Ensure that there are enough copies of the text for each student to see one clearly.
3. Prepare a whiteboard or chart paper for recording group responses.

Steps in Teaching

1. Ask the students to read the first paragraph of text, either aloud or to themselves.
2. Select one student to restate the content of the paragraph in his or her own words.
3. Ask the group of students to determine the key word or words that identify the main point of the paragraph.
4. Record the key word on the board.
5. When all paragraphs have been read, study the list of key words and consider how they have formed a skeleton summary of the text as a whole.

Read and Retell & Key Words

Student Instructions

The Task

You will be required to read a text, piece by piece, and record the key word or words of each paragraph. You will then need to expand upon the key words to create your own simple summary of the text you have read.

Procedure

1. Read the first paragraph of the text.
2. Identify and write the key word or phrase that indicates what that particular paragraph is all about.
3. Expand the key word or words into a full sentence that states what the paragraph was all about.
4. Read the next paragraph of the text.
5. Repeat the process of identifying the key words and expanding them into sentences.
6. Continue the process until all paragraphs have been read and the whole text has been summarized.

Compare and Contrast

Compare and contrast is a strategy that draws students' attention to the ways in which aspects of different texts are alike and different. This strategy can be used to focus attention on the actual content, or the structure, layout and style of the text.

Purpose

This strategy is particularly useful to guide students into focused analysis of a text. It encourages students to look closely at the ways in which aspects are similar or different and enables them to make links between strategies used by authors to communicate the message to the reader.

Steps in Preparation

1. Select two different texts that are in some ways contrasting but which also have similarities.
2. Decide on the aspect of the text to be studied, for example, two different characters in a narrative, two different opinions on an issue, two different formats for presenting the same information.
3. Prepare a Venn diagram, or recording sheet of overlapping circles, or use the blackline master provided on page 92. (See also example on page 67.)

Steps in Teaching

1. As a group, read one of the texts being presented. This can be done independently or by sharing the reading around the group.
2. Discuss the main features of the text according to the focus decided upon by the teacher.
3. Read the second text in the same way as the first.
4. Ask the students to identify any aspects of the two texts that are alike.
5. Record these in the overlapping part of the recording sheet.
6. Ask students to identify any aspects of one text that is not evident in, or is different from, the other text.
7. Record these in the appropriate sections of the sheet.
8. Ask students to think about whether they consider the texts to be more importantly alike or different.

Venn diagram sample: The Logging Dispute

Compare and Contrast

Student Instructions

The Task

You will be asked to read and carefully compare and contrast two texts. In some ways they will be similar, and in other ways there will be obvious differences.

Procedure

1. Read the first text and think carefully about the ways in which the author has expressed ideas and opinions about the central issue or character.
2. Read the second text in the same way.
3. Label the two circles in the recording sheet—one for each text.
4. Consider ways in which the two texts are alike. Record the ways in which they are alike in the overlapping section of the two circles on the recording sheet.
5. In the circle on the left, write down aspects of the first text that are clearly different from the other.
6. Do the same for the other text in the circle on the right.
7. The completed sheet will demonstrate the ways in which the texts are alike and how they are different.

Bundling

Bundling is an activity that helps students identify what they know and to sort this knowledge into a logical sequence. This enables students to respond in writing to a research task.

Purpose

Bundling provides an opportunity for students to list what they know about a research topic. This identifies their concept development and understandings. Each piece of information is written on a separate card. By classifying and sorting the cards the students are bundling together main ideas. This organization of cards is then used to present a written piece of research. The notion of paragraphs becomes very clear through this process. Students begin with words, which become sentences, which become paragraphs, which finally become a detailed and polished piece of writing. This task can be completed with students contributing to the group and producing an information piece as a whole class or individually.

Steps in Preparation

1. Select a topic relevant to the curriculum or students' needs or interests.
2. Prepare cards for recording facts in point form.
3. Ensure that there are some resources available to expand facts if needed.
4. Gather materials for final presentation of research.

Steps in Teaching

1. Identify the topic.
2. Tune the students into the task using a brief discussion to identify some known facts.
3. Students record one fact on each card.
4. Manipulate the cards to bundle related facts together.
5. Expand each bundle into a paragraph using language to link ideas into a cohesive text.
6. The work can remain in this format or be refined as needed.

Bundling sample: The Trojan War

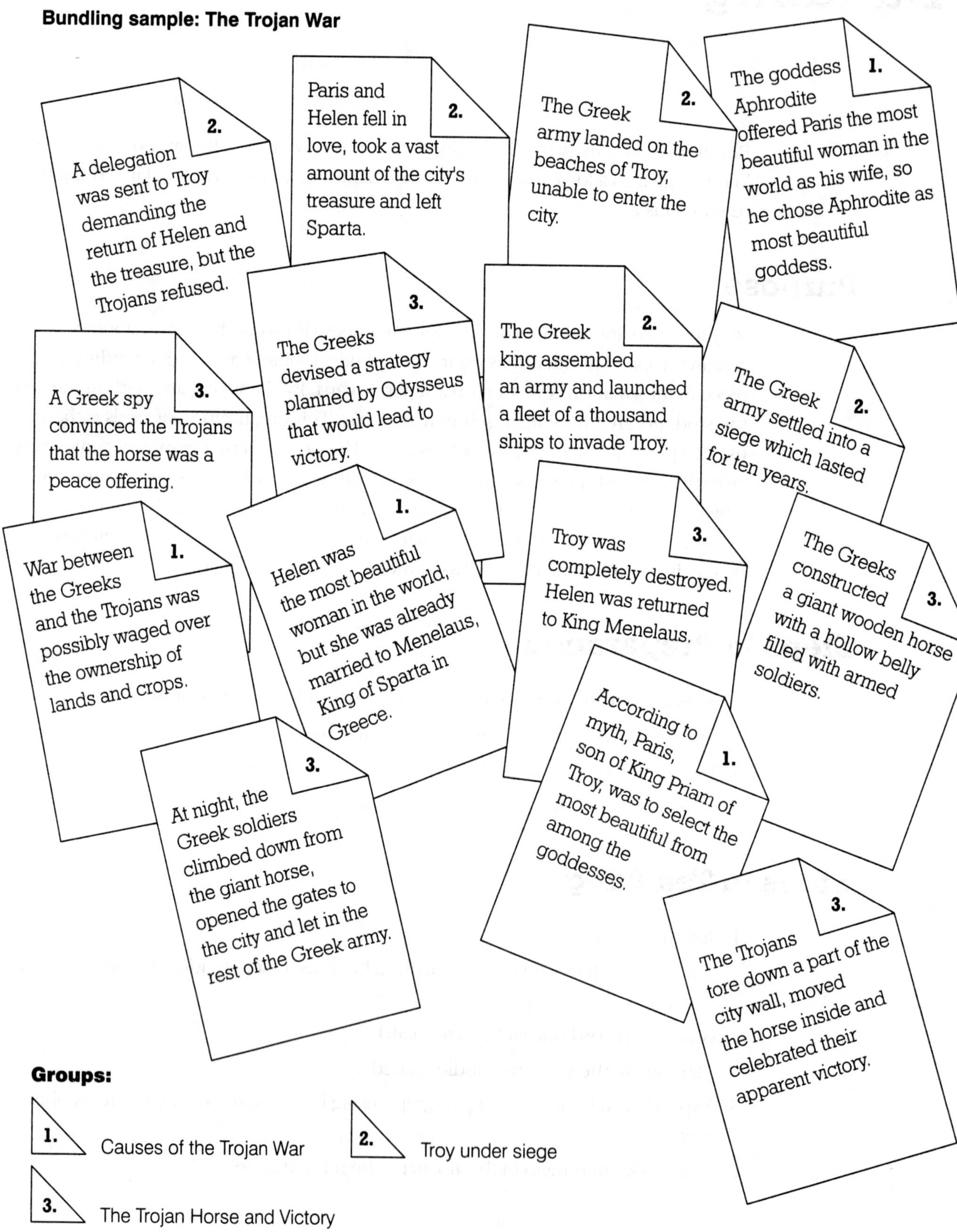

Groups:

1. Causes of the Trojan War

2. Troy under siege

3. The Trojan Horse and Victory

Bundling

Student Instructions

The Task

The task requires you to record on separate cards all the facts you know about a topic. You should then sort the cards into bundles. Each bundle should have facts relating to one idea. When you have finished making the bundles, they can be transformed into paragraphs outlining what you know about each main idea.

Procedure

1. On a single card, record a fact about your topic.
2. Repeat this process of writing a single fact on each new card.
3. Take your cards and sort them into bundles in which the facts in each bundle are all about the same main idea.
4. With your group, discuss reasons for bundling your cards together.
5. Order your bundles into a logical sequence.
6. Select a bundle of cards. Expand each card point into a full sentence.
7. Repeat the process for each card in the bundle.
8. The completed set of sentences may need some word changes to ensure that sentences link together to create a clear paragraph.
9. Repeat this process until you have used all your bundles. You will have created a piece that shows your understandings of the topic.
   Note: At this stage you may need to change the order of paragraphs to make sure the text makes sense as a whole.

Possible Sentences

Students are given a list of words that have been selected from within a piece of expository text. They use these to create sentences that they might expect to find in the text. The students then read through the sentences to ensure they flow well and make up a complete piece of information text. The teacher might choose to show the students the original text so that they can compare their sentences with those created by the author.

Purpose

The purpose of this activity is to give students a supported context in which to generate factual text. It allows teachers to focus on word forms and explore the ways words are changed to keep tense and grammatical conventions intact.

Steps in Preparation

1. Select a piece of text appropriate to student reading levels and curriculum content.
2. Select two or three key words from each sentence and list them together on a sheet.
3. Provide the list of word pairs or groups for students to use.

Steps in Teaching

1. Explain to the students that each pair or group of three words belongs together in one sentence.
2. Discuss the ways that words might need to be changed to ensure consistent and conventional grammar. For example, use suffixes or change tenses of words.
3. Students combine the first group of words into a sentence.
4. Students combine the next group of words into a sentence and ensure that this sentence flows sequentially from the first one.
5. This pattern is continued until all sentences are complete.
6. Read through and edit the whole text to ensure flow and clarity of information.

7. The teacher may decide to give the students a copy of the original text so that a comparison can be made. Students may be surprised by the different ways in which they put their words together, or they may be surprised by how close their sentences correlate to those created by the author. An example is given below.

Possible sentences sample:

Key Words

1. can train, patience
2. Egyptians, 1500 BC
3. small, carnivore
4. vicious, killers, stink
5. smell, glands
6. male, smell, mating
7. glands, remove, vet
8. reqyire care
9. pet, spaying or neutering
10. procedures, healthy animals

FERRETS AS PETS

With patience, you can train ferrets. The Egyptians first kept ferrets as pets in 1500 BC. They are small animals and are carnivorous. They are known as vicious killers and have a reputation for stinking really badly. They smell bad because of the glands found on their bodies. The male has a very strong smell, which is stronger during the mating season. The glands can be removed safely by a trained vet. Keeping them as pets requires care and attention to their needs. If you are going to keep a ferret as a pet, spaying or neutering is advised. If you follow simple hygiene procedures, you can easily keep healthy animals.

Adapted from Stewart, R E 1993, *New Faces: The Complete Book of Alternative Pets,* Agmedia Melbourne

Possible Sentences

Student Instructions

Your teacher may provide you with the original text so that you can compare your text creation with the original.

The Task

You will be given a list of words taken from a factual text. The words are grouped to show you which ones belong together in one sentence. Your task is to write each group of words into a sentence created by you, but that you think could be similar to one written by the original author. As you write each sentence, you will need to take care that it links to the previous sentence and the one to follow. Your complete text should be a sequential, sensible paragraph about a given topic.

You may need to change the grammatical form of a word to make it accurate in your new sentence. For example, you may need to change the tense – for example, "took" instead of "taken". Such grammatical changes are acceptable.

Procedure

1. Look at the heading of your text. You should end up with a paragraph that matches that heading.
2. Take the first pair (or set) of words and combine them into one complete sentence. You will need to imagine what the author might have wanted to say.
3. Look at the next pair (or set) of words. You must repeat the sentence-making process, but ensure that this sentence flows logically from the first one.
4. Continue this process for each set of words provided from the original text.
5. Read through the full paragraph you have written and make sure that it is clear, grammatically correct and easy to follow.

Readers Theatre

Readers theatre is a strategy that enables students to demonstrate their ability to give meaning to text dramatically through the use of words and voice. It may be presented individually or in a group and requires no props or scenery. The main focus is on the presentation of the text.

Purpose

Readers' theatre engages students in text and allows them opportunity to demonstrate their understanding of vocabulary, syntax and meaning, and the forms and functions of language. It also provides students with opportunities to enjoy language and to perform with the support of a group.

Steps in Preparation

1. Discuss play scripts and their layout with the students prior to introducing the readers' theatre activity.
2. Select a text appropriate to the age and reading ability of the group, and suitable for readers'theatre.
3. Reproduce the section of text on an overhead projector sheet or on large posters.

Steps in Teaching

1. Read the text with students a number of times to enable them to become familiar with the storyline. The reading may be done as a whole group or individually.
2. Discuss the text to ensure students have grasped its meaning.
3. The group edits the text in order for it to become a play script. This will require character names to be listed in the left column, direct speech to be quoted, and any stage directions to be placed inside brackets. (See the example on page 76.)
4. Students are allowed time to decide characters and roles and then rehearse their presentation.
5. Performing the text for another group of students is vital to establish purpose. This may be for the class group, other classes or younger students.
6. Allow sharing time after the activity for peer feedback or for students to discuss their own part in the performance and ways performances can be improved in the future.

I helped her carry the shopping bags into the kitchen, dumping them heavily onto the benches. Without trying to put anything away, she walked into the lounge room and slumped down into the only decent chair we had. "It doesn't go very far, you know, Peter,' she told me.

She meant our money, of course, and I felt pleased suddenly that I might be starting a job.

'Any luck with the Scratch lottery ticket, Mum?' I asked hopefully. There wasn't much point. The girls would have told me by now if we'd won anything. But that wasn't really why I was asking.

'No, Peter. I forgot again.'

I knew it. She'd forgotten last week and the week before as well. If I didn't remember for her, she'd never buy one.

'Maybe it's because it's a form of gambling that I forget, Peter.'

Here we go again, I thought. We'd had this argument plenty of times before. "Mum, it's not really gambling. Not like Dad. It's just one dollar. One dollar and no more. We agreed, right? Just one ticket each week.'

'I'm sorry, Peter, I forgot. I'll get it next time I go shopping.'

Source: Moloney, J 1999, *Swashbuckler*, University of Queensland Press, St Lucia Qld

(Sound of walking and dumping bags.)
(Peter helps Mum carry the shopping bags into the kitchen, dumping them heavily onto the benches. Without trying to put anything away, Mum walks into the lounge room and slumps down into the only decent chair.)

MUM (sounding tired):	It doesn't go very far, you know, Peter.
PETER (thinking):	She means our money, of course. I'm pleased that I might be starting a job.
PETER (hopefully):	Any luck with the Scratch lottery ticket, Mum?
PETER (thinking)(aside):	There wasn't much point. The girls would have told me by now if we'd won anything. But that wasn't really why I was asking.
MUM:	No Peter. I forgot again.
PETER (thinking):	I knew it. She forgot last week and the week before as well. If I didn't remember for her, she'd never buy one.
MUM:	Maybe it's because it's a form of gambling that I forget, Peter.
PETER (thinking):	Here we go again.
PETER:	Mum, it's not really gambling. Not like Dad. It's just one dollar. One dollar and no more. We agreed, right? Just one ticket each week.
MUM:	I'm sorry, Peter, I forgot. I'll get it next time I go shopping.

Readers Theatre

Student Instructions

The Task

In this task you will be following up the class reading of the text. You will need to rewrite the text as a formal play script. Roles will need to be assigned to group members. The group should discuss the text and practise performing the play. This activity concludes with a performance of the script your group has prepared.

Procedure

1. Read the text thoroughly.
2. Identify the characters and list their names. You may need to include a narrator.
3. Rewrite the text so that character names appear in the left-hand column, while the actual words they speak appear to the right.
4. Place any instructions to the actors in brackets with their spoken parts.
5. Design roles for the students in your group.
6. Read the text, with group members each reading their roles.
7. Discuss how the text might be performed and enhanced without props or scenery. Discuss the message you want to get across to the other students.
8. Practise your performance, giving feedback to group members.
9. Perform.

Reading Reflection

Reading reflection involves students responding to a piece of text they have read. A written response is usually complete after students have had the opportunity to discuss the text and its elements.

Purpose

A reading reflection provides teachers with indicators of individual student comprehension of a piece of text. It also provides information beyond the literal level, looking into text interpretation and inference. A written reflection offers students an opportunity to respond emotionally. Narrative evokes a range of emotional responses and allows understandings of issues to be clarified.

Steps in Preparation

1. Select a piece of text in which students have been actively engaged. This may be a current novel or class serial story.
2. Prepare questions for students that will lead them beyond literal comprehension of a text. Such questions assist students in organizing their thoughts and responses to their reading. Examples of questions are supplied with the students' instructions.

Steps in Teaching

1. Ensure that enough of the content has been read by the students to enable them to respond.
2. Initiate group discussion that identifies the basic storyline.
3. Discuss the text further, looking at plot complications and resolutions.
4. Discuss:
   - how the story may have changed with different resolutions;
   - the emotions of the story;
   - how the story made the students feel;
   - what students would have done in a similar situation;
   - where character development may be leading.
5. Provide adequate time for students to think and respond.
6. Discuss responses within the groups.

Reading Reflection

Student Instructions

The Task

A reading reflection is your written response to a piece of text you have read. Discussion must take place after reading to help you clarify ideas. You will be expected to look beyond retelling what you have read and be asked to express feelings and opinions.

Procedure

1. Read the text independently.
2. Discuss the text with your group.
3. Complete a written reflection on the piece. The following questions may be helpful in guiding your writing:
   - How did the text make you feel?
   - How would you have handled the situations in the text?
   - What did you think and feel about the characters?
   - In what ways are you alike and different from the main characters?
   - What message do you think the author is trying to convey?
   - Where do you think the story might go from here?
4. Edit and proofread your own work to ensure a flow of ideas and correct grammar and punctuation.
5. Get together with your group and share and discuss your responses.

Conclusion

Building a successful learning community begins with establishing positive relationships in the classroom. A warm, caring atmosphere where children feel secure and free to learn requires mutual respect, ownership, responsibility, and cooperation.

Teachers can provide students with genuine opportunities for thoughtful dialogue and interaction through collaborative learning tasks, from creating a classroom code to developing strategic language skills. Many teachers embrace the "learning centre" style of teaching that helps create a strong educational community.

Establishing independent learning centres where students can work cooperatively in small groups requires careful planning. Experience often leads teachers through curriculum planning and classroom organization when establishing group work. The pages of this book are filled with practical guidelines for classroom organization and instruction all teachers can use when planning, monitoring and facilitating independent learning centres. Establishing the routines and imparting the working skills and behaviors that students will need to use in learning centres are important steps in organizing group work. As students learn to work with others, they begin to take responsibility for their own learning and become considerate of the needs of others.

Working with others allows teachers and students to build relationships, establish trust, create positive environments, acquire knowledge, build language skills, and get to know themselves as learners. To promote self-awareness, students often require supportive strategies that challenge them to contemplate their learning, acknowledge their strengths, accept their limitations and plan their future growth. Effective assessment practices like reflection, goal setting and self-assessment have become important steps in the learning process. Through self-assessment, students can make critical judgements of their work in an effort to grow and improve. The reflective strategies offered in this resource provide a realistic structure for students to set, monitor and evaluate their goals so they can understand and extend the ways they learn.

Successful classrooms are created through the interconnection of many components. The learning community, curriculum, teaching model and assessment practices can influence the daily experiences provided to children. This resource provides both a source and springboard of practical ideas for the learning activities teachers can design for their students. By reflecting on effective teaching practices and considering the needs of students in the classroom, teachers can successfully implement the teaching model and guidelines offered here, modify the strategies and/or refine the ideas to make them their own. Successful classrooms often become exceptional learning communities where ordinary daily activities are shaped into inspiring learning experiences that arouse a sense of passion and enthusiasm for teaching and learning. As Stephanie Harvey writes: "Sharing passion builds community (too).

Blackline Masters

- Goal Setting Steps
- Self-evaluation Survey
- Self-evaluation Checklist for Written Narrative
- Self-evaluation Guide
- Work Sample
- Peer Assessment for Public Speech
- Concept Map
- Data Chart
- Note-taking Scaffold
- Compare and Contrast

Goal Setting and Reflection

Step 1

Setting a goal

- Choose a curriculum context for the goal
- Choose a time frame
- Record the goal

Step 2

Identifying learning strategies to make the goal happen

Step 3

Making a plan

- Select strategies
- Document the plan

Step 4

Keeping the goal in focus

- Display goal in the classroom
- Identify possible obstacles

Step 5

Revisiting and evaluating the goal

- Oral reflection
- Written reflection

Self-evaluation Survey

Name: ______________________________ **Date:** ______________

ENGLISH

Reads for enjoyment
1 2 3 4 5

Reading skills
1 2 3 4 5

Reading comprehension
1 2 3 4 5

Speaking and listening
1 2 3 4 5

Handwriting
1 2 3 4 5

Writes for enjoyment
1 2 3 4 5

Spelling
1 2 3 4 5

Punctuation
1 2 3 4 5

Grammar
1 2 3 4 5

Strengths, and things to work on:

MATH

Tables
1 2 3 4 5

Number work
1 2 3 4 5

Measurement
1 2 3 4 5

Statistics and data
1 2 3 4 5

Space
1 2 3 4 5

Automatic response
1 2 3 4 5

Strengths, and things to work on:

SCIENCE / SOCIAL STUDIES
(Studies of society and environment, Science, Technology, and Health)

Finishes work on time
1 2 3 4 5

Can use a variety of resources
1 2 3 4 5

Presents information in a variety of ways
1 2 3 4 5

Interested in current events
1 2 3 4 5

Strengths, and things to work on:

THE ARTS

Participation
1 2 3 4 5

Work production
1 2 3 4 5

Strengths, and things to work on:

LANGUAGES

Can understand work
1 2 3 4 5

Able to converse
1 2 3 4 5

Strengths, and things to work on:

INFORMATION TECHNOLOGY

Attitude to using computers
1 2 3 4 5

Skills
1 2 3 4 5

Confidence with multimedia
1 2 3 4 5

Confidence using the Internet
1 2 3 4 5

PHYS. ED. AND SPORT

Participation
1 2 3 4 5

Skills
1 2 3 4 5

Enjoyment
1 2 3 4 5

Ability
1 2 3 4 5

Sports participation
1 2 3 4 5

Strengths, and things to work on:

PERSONAL DEVELOPMENT

Cooperation
1 2 3 4 5

Able to take responsibility
1 2 3 4 5

Well organized
1 2 3 4 5

Completes work
1 2 3 4 5

Finishes homework
1 2 3 4 5

Takes care and pride in work
1 2 3 4 5

Takes a leadership role
1 2 3 4 5

General strengths and areas needing work:

Self-evaluation Checklist for Written Narrative

Name of author: ______________________ **Date:** __________

Title of work: ______________________

Genre used: ______________________

Consider and rate your response to the text under the following categories:	1	2	3
Format			
• Page layout including position of words and artwork			
• Choice of appropriate genre, e.g. narrative, procedure, report			
• Presentation of information, e.g. paragraphs, sections			
• Use of different text styles to gain effect, e.g. italics, bold, CAPITALS			
Further comments:			
Tools			
• Use of headings and subheadings			
• Use of appropriate punctuation, e.g. comma (,) quotation marks (" "), colon (:), ellipsis (…)			
• Accuracy of spelling			
• Use of correct grammar, e.g. consistency in tense, direct speech, pronouns			
• Use of dialogue			
Further comments:			
Language			
• Choice of specialized and technical words			
• Use of metaphor, simile, adjective, etc.			
• Use of emotive language, e.g. angry, joyful, anxious, passionate			
• Vivid description of characters to create realistic images			
• Use of the element of surprise or the unexpected to gain reader response			
• Good choice of title			
• Clear development of plot, e.g. events are in order and problems are solved			
Further comments:			
Scale: 1 = little evidence 2 = some evidence 3 = consistently evident			

Self-evaluation Guide

Title: ______________________________

Context:

This piece of work was completed because . . .

Task outline:

The task given to me was to . . .

Judgements:

I am happy with . . .

because . . .

I think it could have been better if . . .

because . . .

Next time I do a task like this I will think more about . . .

Work Sample

Name of author: ______________________ **Date:** __________

Title: ______________________

Context: ______________________

This work was chosen for inclusion in my portfolio because . . .

It shows that I can . . .

It shows that I know about . . .

Peer Assessment for Public Speech

Name: ____________________

Topic: ____________________

Assessed by: ____________________

Scale: ✔ ✔✔ ✔✔✔

Characteristics of a good speech:

Voice

- Clarity
- Volume
- Tone

Content

- Appropriateness
- Interest

Comment:

Concept Map

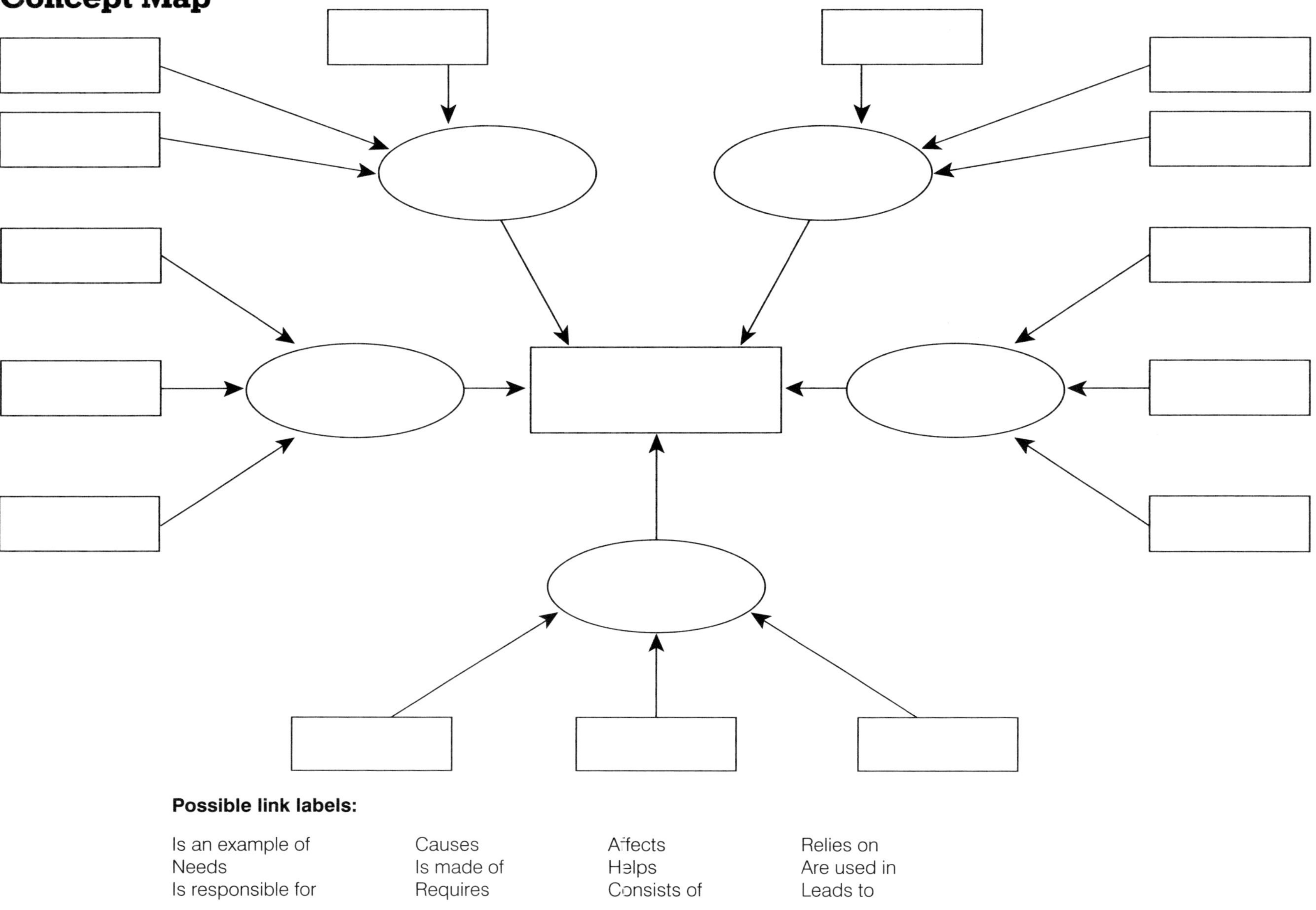

Possible link labels:

Is an example of	Causes	Affects	Relies on
Needs	Is made of	Helps	Are used in
Is responsible for	Requires	Consists of	Leads to

Data Chart

Name: ______________________ **Topic:** ______________________

	Heading:	Heading:	Heading:	Heading:	Heading:
What we already know:					
Resource 1:					
Resource 2:					
Resource 3:					

Note-taking Scaffold

Name: ____________________

Topic: ____________________

Subheading	Detail 1:
	Detail 2:
	Detail 3:
Subheading	Detail 1:
	Detail 2:
	Detail 3:
Subheading	Detail 1:
	Detail 2:
	Detail 3:
Subheading	Detail 1:
	Detail 2:
	Detail 3:

Compare and Contrast

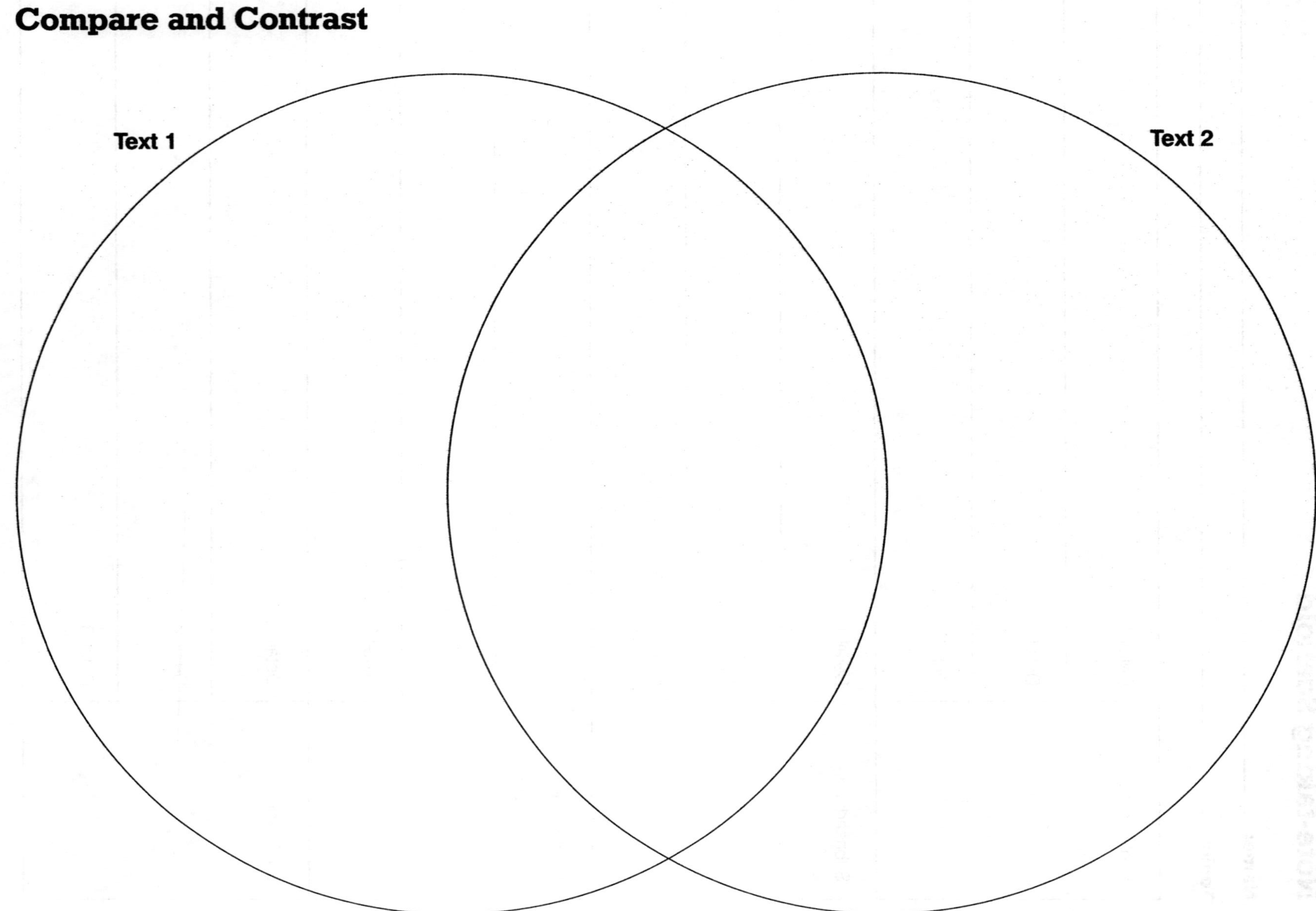

Professional References

Booth, D. *Reading and Writing in the Middle Years*. Markham, Ontario: Pembroke Publishers, 2001.

Boyd, J. and Dalton, J. I *Teach: A Guide to Inspiring Classroom Leadership*. Armadale Vic: Eleanor Curtain Publishing, 1992.

Bridges, L. *Assessment: Continuous Learning*. Portland, Maine: Stenhouse Publishers, 1996.

Bridges, L. *Creating Your Classroom Community*. Portland, Maine: Stenhouse Publishers, 1996.

Brownlie, F. and J. King. *Learning in Safe Schools: Creating Classrooms Where All Students Belong*. Markham, Ontario: Pembroke Publishers, 2000.

Burke, K., R. Fogarty, and S. Belgrad. *The Portfolio Connection: Student Work Linked to Standards, 2nd.ed.* Portsmouth, New Hampshire: Heinemann Publishers, 2001.

Caldwell, J. and Michael P. Ford. *Where Have All the Bluebirds Gone? How to Soar with Flexible Grouping*. Portsmouth, New Hampshire: Heinemann Publishers, 2002.

Cohen, J.H. and R.B. Wiener. *Literacy Portfolios: Improving Assessment, Teaching,and Learning, 2nd ed.* Portsmouth, New Hampshire: Heinemann Publishers, 2002.

Courtney, A.M. and T.L. Abodeeb (ed.) *Journey of Discovery: Building a Classroom Community Through Diagnostic-Reflective Portfolios*. Newark, Delaware: International Reading Association, 2001.

Dalton, J. and Watson, M. *Among Friends: Classrooms where Caring and Learning Prevail*. Armadale Vic: Eleanor Curtain Publishing, 1997.

Daniels H. and M. Bizar. *Methods That Matter: Six Structures for Best Practice Classrooms*. Portland, Maine: Stenhouse Publishers, 1998.

Davies, A. *Making Classroom Assessment Work*. Merville, British Columbia: Connections Publishing, 2000.

Diller, D. *Literacy Work Stations: Making Centres Work*. Portland, Maine: Stenhouse Publishers, 2003.

Easley, S. and K. Mitchell. *Portfolios Matter: What, Where, When, Why, and How to Use Them*. Markham, Ontario: Pembroke Publishers, 2003.

Flippo, R.F. *Assessing Readers: Qualitative Diagnosis and Instruction*. Portsmouth, New Hampshire: Heinemann Publishers, 2003.

Fogarty, R. *Balanced Assessment*. Portsmouth, New Hampshire: Heinemann Publishers, 1998.

Forster, M. and Masters, G. *Portfolios: Assessment Resource Kit*. Camberwell Vic: Australian Coucil for Educational Research, 1996.

Foster, G. *Langugae Arts Idea Bank: Instructional Strategies for Supporting Student Learning*. Markham, Ontario: Pembroke Publishers, 2003.

Glasser, W. *Control Theory in the Classroom*. New York: Harper and Row, 1986.

Gregory, K., C. Cameron, and A. Davies. *Self-Assessment and Goal-Setting*. Merville, British Columbia: Connections Publishing, 2000.

Harvey, S. *Nonfiction Matters: Reading Writing and Research in Grades 3-8*. Portland, Maine: Stenhouse Publishers, 1998.

Hill, S. and Hancock, J. *Reading and Writing Communities—Cooperative Literacy Learning in the Classroom*. Armadale Vic: Eleanor Curtain Publishing, 1993.

Hill, S. and Hill, T. *The Collaborative Classroom—A Guide to Cooperative Learning*. Armadale Vic: Eleanor Curtain Publishing, 1990.

Holt, L. *Snapshots: Literacy Minilessons Up Close*. Portsmouth, New Hampshire: Heinemann Publishers, 2000.

Koechlin, C. and S. Zwaan. *Info Tasks for Successful Learning: Building Skills in Reading, Writing, and Research*. Markham, Ontario: Pembroke Publishers, 2001.

Luongo-Orlando, K. *A Project Approach to Language Learning: Linking Literary Genres and Themes in Elementary Classrooms*. Markham, Ontario: Pembroke Publishers, 2001.

Luongo-Orlando, K. Authentic *Assessment: Designing Performance-Based Tasks*. Markham, Ontario: Pembroke Publishers, 2003.

McGrath, H. and Noble, T. *Different Kids, Same Classroom*. Melbourne, Vic: Longman, 1993.

McMackin, M.C. and B.S. Siegel. *Knowing How: Researching and Writing Non-fiction 3-8*. Portland, Maine: Stenhouse Publishers, 2002.

Miller, D. *Reading With Meaning: Teaching Comprehension in the Primary Grades*. Portland, Maine: Stenhouse Publishers, 2002.

Nagel, G.K. *Effective Grouping for Literacy Instruction*. Portsmouth, New Hampshire: Heinemann Publishers, 2001.

Owochi, G. and Y. Goodman. *Kidwatching: Documenting Children's Literacy Development*. Portsmouth, New Hampshire: Heinemann Publishers, 2002.

Pigdon, K. And Woolley, M. *The Big Picture—Integrating Children's Learning*. Armadale, Vic: Eleanor Curtain Publishing, 1992.

Reid, J., Forrestal, P. and Cook, J. *Small Group Learning in the Classroom*. Rozelle, NSW: Chalkface Press, 1989.

Routman, R. *Conversations: Strategies for Teaching, Learning and Evaluating*. Portsmouth, New Hampshire: Heinemann Publishers, 2000.

Schipper, B. and J. Rossi. *Portfolios in the Classroom:Tools for Mlearning and Instruction*. Portland, Maine: Stenhouse Publishers,1997.

Strickland, K. and J. Strickland. *Making Assessment Elementary*. Portsmouth, New Hampshire: Heinemann Publishers, 2000.

Wilson, J. and Wing Jan, L. *Thinking for Themselves*. Armadale, Vic: Eleanor Curtain Publishing, 1993.

Index